Praise for Get to CEO

"As a tool for mentoring business professionals at any career stage, Hilbrich's timeless inspirations for self-improvement are a benefit to all. John demonstrates a genuine interest in the growth of others by sharing the keen insights that guided his successful career and can transform yours too."

—DANIEL G. DOSTER, CEO PAPER WATER BOTTLE

"Lots of books talk about being a CEO. Not very many show you the path to get there. The simple advice presented is clear, and easy to grasp. I had the privilege to watch John in action as a CEO. His personal stories punctuate an exciting path for aspiring executives. I wish this book had been available to me during my journey."

—KEVIN LAVALLEE,
PRESIDENT AND CEO, THYSSENKRUPP ELEVATOR

"John's practical and insightful advice is backed by years of experience and real-world examples that will help leaders unlock their full potential to make the jump to the C-Suite."

—KELLY COLEMAN,
CEO, HANCOCK ENTERPRISES OIL AND GAS EXPLORATION.

"John has authored a book that is an essential guide on the tenets of leadership and the skills required to achieve and flourish as a CEO. I recommend this book for anyone aspiring to a leadership role."

—FRED KENDALL,
HEAD OF JAPAN IMAGING SERVICES, AMAZON.COM, INC.

"Having experienced working with John in the early years, I can honestly say that his wisdom, practical insights, and true passion make this book a must read for anyone striving for a leadership position."

—KLAUS HAHN, CEO TESTFAKTA GROUP NORDIC AB

"John is a passionate experienced guide, who wants you to win. This book is packed with heart, guidance and hard-won wisdom to help you achieve."

—JON EVANS, CEO NORTH FORK BUILDERS

"I have known John for more than 40 years and admire his passion for living life to the greatest extent possible. His enthusiasm is contagious, and he wants everyone around him to achieve success in their own way. This book provides motivation and practical skills to help you navigate your way to becoming an extraordinary leader."

—JAMES G. HART, PRESIDENT AND CHIEF INVESTMENT OFFICER, OLIVER ESTATE, INC.

"A great read with valuable guidance and insight as to what to do, and maybe more importantly, what not to do in one's quest to become CEO. The author's candor and humility make this a real pleasure to read. I can't wait to give it to my children, for them to absorb and learn as they progress in their efforts to get to CEO."

—CEO, THE LARGEST PRIVATELY OWNED
JEWELRY RETAIL COMPANY IN THE U.S.

"Drawing on his own journey and experience, John offers practical advice and strategies for anyone aspiring to the top job. True to himself, John shares guidance from the heart, some hard earned wisdom and personal anecdotes that should prove to be valuable insight to others".

—JOE CHESHAM, PRESIDENT,
PRIME COMMUNICATIONS CANADA

"John's book „Get to CEO" is a very well crafted description of a career path that he followed successfully. He illustrates clear and empathetically what helped him and will help young, dynamic and committed people to become equally successful. Apart from his very good, intuitive understanding of client's needs, knowing the facts and data, he always showed an enormous empathy and support for his co-workers. The team building skills helped him to move forward, to become a trusted department head and finally CEO. I believe young people can learn a lot from his book for their own ambitious career."

—ACHIM SCHULZ, DIRECTOR,
MICHAEL CONRAD & LEO BURNETT GERMANY

"This book will encourage your heart and show you the way in your next steps to becoming a CEO. John's guidance is an invaluable resource in building the skills you will need to succeed in either a large or small company."

—MARK SPRINGER, CEO, DAYSPRING RESTORATION

"John has hit on some of the top points and competencies that make a successful leader. Sharing his experience and his personal stories of success and failure make the reading of his book entertaining as well as insightful. If you're a leader looking for ideas to elevate your skills and behavior, I highly recommend this read."

—SCOTT ROBINSON,
MANAGING DIRECTOR, ROBINSON RESOURCE GROUP

"I have worked with Hilbrich for decades, and I am not surprised that I continue to learn from the gems in this book. John wants to inspire you to the top job. These pages are packed with the real world advice you need to help you reach your goals in business."

—STEPHEN SIMMONS,
PRESIDENT, CEO, TNG FINANCIAL SOFTWARE INC.

CEO's are always in the news. Much is written about them. But the path to get to the top job is a mystery. John guides you on a simple journey, presented in a clear, coaching style. His personal stories add empathy and authenticity as he helps aspiring executives avoid the pitfalls on the exciting path to CEO.

—MAX SCHEDER-BIESCHIN,
FOUNDER, CEO, BOARD MEMBER

"In a very practical style, filled with wisdom, deeply personal stories and passion, John provides a wealth of practical insights on what it takes to be a successful leader, and get to CEO."

—ROBERT HASHIMOTO, CEO, THINK LOGISTICS

"It's not easy being CEO. It's also not an obvious path to navigate your way to the top job. John helps you solve both of those challenges by providing guidance on the journey and a clear picture of the skills necessary to be a success."

—JOE BRANDT, PRESIDENT, CARDINAL DISTRIBUTING CO.

"Contrary to everything we are fed in the media, being the CEO is not a glamorous job. There are real internal conflicts and decisions are not easy. As a society we spend so much time referencing the exceptions (Musk, Bezos, Zuckerberg, Jobs, Gates) that we neglect the people aspiring to the job and succeeding everyday. Aspiring leaders can find mentors and role models in their own communities and in John's book."

—MARK ANTHONY, CEO, ENTREPRENEUR

"Whether the company is large and small, this book will help the next generation of leaders focus on what's important to thrive. John's book is a must read on the key tenets of leadership and the skill development required to achieve and flourish in the top job."

—BLAKE UNDERRINER, MANAGING PARTNER, UNDERRINER AUTOMOTIVE

"I had the great pleasure to watch John in action when we were both relatively early in our executive roles. Even then John stood out in our circle of CEOs with a warm smile and quick mind that lit up every room he graced. "Get to CEO" captures John's wisdom earned through his CEO journey. If you have the fire to start your own journey, then "Get to CEO" is a must-read."

—MICHAEL MEAGHER, CEO AND SERIAL ENTREPRENEUR

"Unprecedented times require a new approach by future leaders. John's personal and touching stories invite us to look at how we should construct a new way of working and leading. "Get to CEO" is a perfect guide to become a better leader and transform "business as usual" into a path to find win-win-win approachs to benefit organizations, customers, and our larger society."

—FRANK EIGLER, CEO EIGLER COMMUNICATIONS

"John has always had the knowledge of not only what it takes to be a CEO but also the path required to become CEO. He is a true communicator and this book will be perfect for those interested in the journey to become a CEO. John has always mentored those around him thru sharing his experiences. He has the unique ability to put into words what is required to achieve a specific goal. These insights are so important to those seeking a path to success."

—PETER GARVY, PRESIDENT, LIFESPICE

"I have known John a long-time and this book is a reflection of his commitment to others in their personal and professional growth, his insightful and practical approach to setting oneself up for success, and John's acute awareness of the need to have a holistic approach to leadership in order to thrive."

—BILL BEST, FOUNDER & CEO GARRETT LANE ADVISORS

"John is a passionate, experienced guide, who wants you to win. This book is packed with heart, guidance and hard-won wisdom to help you achieve."

—RICK UNGERSMA, PRESIDENT & CEO, MURDOCH'S RANCH & HOME SUPPLY

"If you or someone you know are serious about getting to the top job, this book is an invaluable read. John provides the path in a very practical approach and fills the pages with stories, anecdotes and the common struggles of the journey."

—ED BENFORD, CEO BENFORD CAPITAL PARTNERS

Accolades for "Get to CEO" are well deserved. John is a great person, a great family man and CEO.

—MATTHEW J. ALAGNA JR., FOUNDER AND CEO, ALL TRUCK TRANSPORTATION CO. INC.

GET TO CEO

GET TO CEO

JOHN HILBRICH

NEW DEGREE PRESS

COPYRIGHT © 2023 JOHN HILBRICH

All rights reserved.

GET TO CEO

ISBN   979-8-88926-927-4 *Paperback*
        979-8-88926-807-9 *Hardcover*
        979-8-88926-970-0 *Ebook*

Dedication

This book is dedicated to my wife, Sue, and my children, Jack, Annika, Tom, Christian, Sanne, and Nicholette. If not for your deep love, support, and "Let's go for it!" adventurous spirit, not one of my experiences would have happened, nor would one word of this book have been written.

Contents

DEDICATION 13
EPIGRAPH 17

INTRODUCTION 19

PART I. **SELF AWARENESS** **25**
CHAPTER 1. GOALS 29
CHAPTER 2. REALISTICALLY ASSESS YOUR SKILLS 37
CHAPTER 3. WHAT IS YOUR SUPERPOWER? 43
CHAPTER 4. WHAT DOES SUCCESS MEAN TO YOU? 47
CHAPTER 5. WHAT DRIVES YOUR SUCCESS? 53
CHAPTER 6. HOW DO YOU INFLUENCE OTHERS? 61

PART II. **PERFORMANCE ROUTINE** **65**
CHAPTER 7. WHAT IS YOUR SIGNATURE? 69
CHAPTER 8. ESTABLISH HIGHLY PRODUCTIVE ROUTINES 77
CHAPTER 9. LEARN AND DON'T STOP LEARNING 89
CHAPTER 10. PAUSE AND REFLECT 97
CHAPTER 11. DON'T BE THE SMARTEST PERSON IN THE ROOM 103
CHAPTER 12. MEASURE YOUR PERFORMANCE 111
CHAPTER 13. GETTING UNSTUCK 119

PART III. **RUN TO THE FIRE** **125**
CHAPTER 14. WHAT DOES IT MEAN TO RUN TO THE FIRE? 129
CHAPTER 15. WHICH FIRES DO I RUN TO? 137

CHAPTER 16.	CHOOSE YOUR TEAM CAREFULLY	141
CHAPTER 17.	SAY YES AND FIGURE IT OUT	147
CHAPTER 18.	CONFRONT STUFF, LOOK AROUND CORNERS, AND BELIEVE	157
CHAPTER 19.	YOU MUST BE NUTS	163

PART IV.	**MANAGE UP**	**169**
CHAPTER 20.	DON'T LET YOUR EGO GET THE BEST OF YOU	173
CHAPTER 21.	KNOW YOUR NUMBERS	179
CHAPTER 22.	ARE YOU A THREAT?	185

PART V.	**SERVE OTHERS**	**191**
CHAPTER 23.	INSPIRING OTHERS	199
CHAPTER 24.	REMEMBER YOU ARE HUMAN	205
CHAPTER 25.	BE READY TO LEAD	213
CHAPTER 26.	SEE THE FUTURE AND PAINT THE PICTURE	235
CHAPTER 27.	THE HELPLESS CEO	243

START YOUR JOURNEY READING LIST	251
ACKNOWLEDGMENTS	255
APPENDIX	259

Epigraph

―――

What most people fear makes few people great.

Introduction

To achieve the results that only 5 percent of the population has, you have to have the guts to do what the other 95 percent are unwilling to do.

—ROBIN SHARMA

I have always been struck by this quote.

It reframes my thinking. I always thought of success in terms of the things that I had to do. Tasks I had to accomplish to get ahead. Plans I had to make. Chances I had to take.

I only understood later in life that I got ahead because I did things others weren't doing or weren't willing to do. I took on projects others didn't want. I went into the office on Sunday mornings at half past four while my family slept. I got on planes to take care of clients when others thought it unnecessary. I chose to take challenging roles in foreign countries while others called me nuts to uproot my family, learn a new language, and seek success. The risk could have derailed my career. What happens if I failed, and the company doesn't have a role for me when I come back?

Although I heard Robin Sharma utter those words later in my career, I had already engaged in his advice. Maybe that's why I cherish the quote and why it struck me as truth.

I want to help you realize this truth as you read this book.

You are reading this book because you are an aspiring leader, interested in learning how to get to the top faster. You want to become the CEO, acquire the skills and habits to get there, and avoid the pitfalls in the process. The trek to CEO isn't very clear. Whether you are navigating your career in a large organization or acquiring the skills in a smaller company, getting to the top job isn't an obvious, well-worn path.

Talk to any CEO. The path to get the job creates uncertainty and risk—and careers are often humbled with failure and personal sacrifice. But CEOs have one thing in common: They persevered, kept moving forward, created opportunities where they could, and developed their own methods of success.

Studies of CEOs have shown that the path isn't always straight up (Botelho, 2018). Sometimes you must go sideways to get ahead. Sometimes you must take a role where you learn skills you don't have so that you can move forward. Sometimes sticking your neck out, failing, learning, and sitting on the sidelines to wait for another shot is necessary.

Achievers understand this. Climbing the ladder of life, entrepreneurship, parenthood, business, or academia is never a linear upward ascent. Though it might sound frustrating, the nonlinear nature of some of these experiences is where we learn the most and become the most patient, observant, and understanding of others. Rather than simply driving hard all the time, we learn to slow down, listen, understand others, and grow in our wisdom and leadership.

Mark Zuckerberg, accused of stealing the idea for Facebook from two Harvard classmates, overcame the hurdles and has built a global social media organization. Jeff Bezos, rejected by twenty-three venture capital firms, went on to found and lead Amazon to greatness. Oprah Winfrey, fired from her first television job as a news anchor, went on to create the most watched talk show on television and build a media empire. Steve Jobs, fired from Apple, the company he founded, experienced startup failure with NeXT prior to coming back to Apple and creating the iPhone, iMac, iPod, and iPad.

In addition to learning from failure and fostering the skills necessary for success, they learned to persevere—doing things others were unwilling to do.

The path to CEO isn't obvious because you can't get there via just the nine to five. Sure, you need to excel in your daily work. But that's only the basic 95 percent effort required to get you to CEO. The other 5 percent, the 5 percent that gets you the job, is in personal development: getting up early to think and plan, taking the tough projects others won't, putting yourself at risk where your peers aren't willing. As you take on these and several other critical responsibilities, you will watch your peers fall away and not engage for several reasons: They have other priorities. They don't want to commit to the time. They are completely risk-averse. They could also be just plain scared.

And, unfortunately, as you will read in my personal stories later, you may be ridiculed for doing what it takes. As you begin to do this, it will become obvious, as you watch others, that you are doing the things they aren't willing to do. In its best sense, it can create personal power for you.

A path to acquiring the skills, mindset, habits, and leadership orientation necessary for getting to CEO exists, although it isn't obvious. I will show you how self-awareness—understanding how you operate and are perceived by others—is paramount in your journey. You will learn how to perform in your roles and get credit for accomplishments. Taking risks (an important part of career advancement), learning, and launching to greater confidence are calibrated opportunities that one must learn to master. Do you really know how you are being measured? You will learn how to understand this concept and make it work for you and others. I will lead you through my failure with one of the most important concepts in business: managing up. Lastly, you can't get ahead without others. How you serve others greatly dictates how they will serve you.

I have been a CEO for over twenty-five years, in large and small organizations, as a professional manager and entrepreneur. Having lived in five countries with my family and managed people through my business career in seventeen countries, I have had countless amazing experiences and suffered many failures, often far from home. I got my first top management job at thirty-three years old running a foreign office at a global advertising agency. I felt confident but scared to death and had no idea how to address the team. Little did I know, those were the least of my problems.

I have grown businesses ten times in size, navigated turnarounds, acquired global companies, and started companies from scratch. I have seen a lot in my career. Some of it I prepared for. Much I did not. But I fostered the ability to fall back on the learning pillars of success, failure, and experience to fashion a plan.

I will share many personal stories of the problems I faced, my successful solutions, and my struggles. You will see that my wife and family played an important role in my career, both in the joy and, sometimes, the suffering.

I would like you to emerge, having read this book, with your own plan to get to CEO. I will show you the blueprint to develop the skill set, avoid the pitfalls, and move forward confidently. To help you take action to develop your own plan, I have included a "Quick Coaching Session" at the end of each chapter to get you there faster.

Becoming a CEO is a realistic, chartable opportunity if you follow the path. I hope through sharing forty years of global business, personal development, and leadership experience, you will be well equipped to begin a successful journey to get to CEO.

PART ONE

SELF AWARENESS

When talking about getting "there," defining "there" is important. Have you set a goal? Do you want to gain an important opportunity, promotion, or some achievement of success? Do you want a happy marriage? Do you want to lose fifteen pounds? Getting there faster is about knowing where you're going. And the only way to know where you're going is to be aware—self-aware—of where you are.

Doing your own self-assessment is important. How do I feel about where I am today? What do I want to achieve tomorrow, a month from now, and a year from now? Where am I stuck? What is slowing me down? How happy am I, really? How happy are those around me who I care about? Do I feel like I'm really on the right path? Am I growing fast enough and getting noticed and promoted in my work?

The answers to these questions, and others you will certainly come up with yourself, are key to understanding where you are today. You can only set goals for where you want to be tomorrow when you understand where you are today. Self-awareness is a broad, all-encompassing term. For our purposes, I would like to simplify it. Where are you today? Where would you like to go tomorrow? It's about how you feel about yourself now and how you would like to feel about yourself in the future. It's about how you walk into a room and how you are perceived by others.

A deep understanding of these phenomena will help you recognize your skills, your confidence level, how much you are truly capable of, and most importantly, it will help you gain access to your superpowers. We will dig into each of these in Part One to help you become more self-aware and take the first steps toward getting to CEO.

CHAPTER 1

Goals

A goal properly set is halfway reached.
—ZIG ZIGLAR

My biggest career mistake? I never wrote my goals down.

I always thought, *I've got my goals in my head.* While mostly true, they were not focused and admittedly unclear. I would often lose sight of them. When they are written down, you can revisit them. You can work from them. You can ideate from them, and you know where to go each day to look at them. You know where they are, and you know what they are. Otherwise, you roll into your office, and you take on whatever it is that happened to hit you that day or overnight.

Early in my career, I worked for a large global advertising agency. I had accepted a transfer from Chicago to Frankfurt, Germany—a big opportunity! My wife Sue and I, who now have a large family together, were childless at the time. Over the five years living in Frankfurt, we celebrated having three children. Professionally, during that time, promotions came fast and furious. The company grew, and I grew with it. To continue my growth, an opportunity came up to move from Frankfurt to Copenhagen to take over one of the European offices there.

To complicate matters, Sue and I had many discussions about transferring back to the US to afford the grandparents more time to spend with the grandkids.

In one conversation, Sue pushed me on what my goals were. To be honest, I'd never thought about specific goals. I chased the ladder. I chased challenges. I helped my clients. And all of it seemed to be going in the right direction for me. I received many promotions, and now I had a great opportunity to run an office in Copenhagen. What's the big deal?

Our discussions got more intense.

Why didn't I have goals? Where are we going as a family? Why didn't I plan for us, versus having the company make the decisions? These were good questions.

Unfortunately, I hadn't considered them much. Sue always thought things over deeply because she would have to bear the large burden of moving our family, working through finding a new place to live, finding doctors, figuring out the language, and doing simple things like grocery shopping—typically while I worked.

More importantly, she prompted me to dig for answers because she had a career prospect. She had been offered a position as the first special education teacher at the Frankfurt

International School. This role went beyond teaching—Sue would be crafting the entire FIS Special Education Program. She had gone back to school and worked hard to get her MEd Special Education in Learning Disabilities and Behavior Disorders. Her degree, experience, and expertise created this potent opportunity to get back into teaching in a significant way. A move would mean she would have to decline the offer. This weighed heavily on me.

I needed to get my act together to better enunciate my goals and aspirations while taking a more active role in designing my professional life.

We decided, together, to make that next move to Copenhagen. Sue recognized the opportunity for my career and our family, and she turned down the teaching job of a lifetime. This would not be the last time she demonstrated such selflessness.

She also remained relentless in her pursuit of keeping me honest with my goals.

She asked, "Is this your dream? Or is it your employer's dream that you are participating in?"

Were they determining my future?

At the time, our dreams were connected, I think. I performed, created opportunity, and they saw it the same way. When things are good, everything goes in the right direction for everyone. But things aren't always good. That's why goals are so important. Sue pushed me, and it got me thinking about my specific goals for the first time.

Five years later—after a couple more corporate moves and some difficulty in navigating the organization's politics—my goals no longer meshed with those of the company. Having spent more time thinking, goal setting, and contemplating what I wanted and what worked best for my family, leaving the company made sense.

Had I not spent the time thinking about what I wanted and what my family needed, I would have been stuck—and miserable. Fortunately, as I began to recognize the unhappiness in my work, the reasons for getting stuck were clear: I did not enjoy the work as I once did. I couldn't flourish. I couldn't lead like I knew I should. The opportunities that got me there didn't exist anymore. I only came to this recognition because I had a better idea of what I wanted and knew to be most important. Had I not known, I would have been stuck and miserable in a dead-end job. Having been stuck before, I understood this in my gut. But clarity existed because I spent the necessary time thinking about my goals and how to get them.

Live and learn.

You must commit. You must write goals down. Many have goals but never put pen to paper. If you don't formally commit to them, they are difficult to achieve. If you don't repeat them daily and believe you can achieve them, you will experience amorphous moments when you believe you are trying to achieve something but it's wildly unspecific. It won't have an end date or a target. You won't be focused in your thinking about how to achieve it. Worst of all, the "goals" floating in your head will constantly change with the wind. You will become a slave to whatever seems important in the moment, forsaking big opportunities for small fires and cheating your potential.

Can you tell I am passionate about getting you on the goal-setting train?

Goal setting takes some work but is a complete necessity. Goals are best when specific and measurable and written down. You may have heard of SMART goals (Doran 1981).

SMART means goals should be specific, measurable, assignable, realistic, and time-related. The acronym creates a clear and simple framework. When setting goals, keeping things brief is best. Any more than five goals is just a task list. Task lists should be avoided. Goals are big, important, noteworthy events that will measure something in your life when you achieve them. Being able to sit in a quiet room, think about and enunciate your goals, and write them down is the first step. The second step is to read through them every day—without fail.

When I approach this process, I try to think through five important achievements that I would like to tackle over the next twelve months. These are simple, yearly goals. I learned this process from Robin Sharma in his book *The 5AM Club*. Staying simple and thinking through what the achievement of these goals will get you provides so much opportunity.

Once you have written down five simple, important goals, the next step is to plot the path to achieving them. Break goal achievement and strategies down into ninety-day increments.

Look at your five goals and write down a maximum of ten tasks or strategies—two to three per goal that are clear tasks and direct paths toward achieving those goals. Again, be specific and measurable when it comes to the tasks. Revisit them daily, or at minimum weekly, in terms of your daily schedule or weekly organizational plan.

Linking your goals together with your daily tasks—so that 80 percent of your time is spent on achieving your top goals, while 20 percent is spent on daily administration—is important. If you spend the bulk of your time on your most important activities and minimize time simply being busy with less important administrative duties, you will knock your goals down much more effectively.

Those goals must make a big difference in your professional and personal life, or they shouldn't be on the list. If they are designed to create success, you should be spending 80 percent of your time on them.

Big goal equals big action.

Grant Cardone's book, *The 10X Rule*, is a great motivational tool related to goal setting. Goal setting is an interesting psychological phenomenon. Because most people don't want to fail, they set goals that are "achievable." They don't recognize that they are limiting themselves. If you set goals at ten times what you think you can achieve, yes, there's a chance you may not hit that number. But my guess is you will go far beyond what you achieve versus just setting something that you knew you could handle.

Another interesting psychological pitfall that happens in goal setting is that folks reduce goals that seem too high or too hard. What good is a goal if you were not pushing yourself far beyond what you normally would do to achieve it? If you reduce it because it might seem that it's unachievable, what good is that?

It's like cheating at golf. You are only fooling yourself.

Seriously, setting big goals is important because big goals beget big action. And when you get big action, you are going to go beyond the boundaries of what you might have done. Yes, you may make big mistakes. But big goals can't be achieved without those big mistakes. And guess what? You learn big from big mistakes, which will help you achieve bigger goals.

QUICK COACHING SESSION:

1. Write down your five big goals for the coming twelve-month period. Think of them in terms of your personal and professional life.

   _____
   _____
   _____
   _____
   _____
   _____

2. Now sequence your way to achieving those goals on a monthly basis. What do you need to get done over the next three, six, nine, and twelve months to achieve those goals?

   _____
   _____
   _____
   _____
   _____
   _____

3. Do you have a story where you achieved success because you had a goal and stuck to it? Write it down in a journal, and keep building on it by setting more goals and achieving them.

   _____
   _____
   _____
   _____
   _____
   _____

CHAPTER 2

Realistically Assess Your Skills

Knowing yourself is the beginning of all wisdom.
—ARISTOTLE

When I mentor leaders on assessing their skills, I ask them to remember learning how to ride a bike.

Once you figured it out, you were psyched to go out and ride it every day. You got better and better at it. You continued to improve by riding faster and bigger bikes over different terrains. You mastered the art of riding a bike, as long as the bike had two wheels.

Now, can you ride a unicycle?

A big part of achieving goals is understanding your skills. A truthful, humble skills assessment is necessary to understand the tools you have to get there faster. Are you people-oriented?

To understand your superpower, you need to consider a few things:

1. What makes you stand out? In situations at home, with friends, or at work, where have you excelled? Have you ever stood out, been awarded, or achieved a level that surpassed others?
2. Once you understand what has made you stand out from others over the course of your life, link some skills to what has made you successful. What specific skills have you developed that make you stand out above the competition? How did you get those skills? How long and hard did you work at them? Now you are more aware of what makes you special and how you got there.
3. Now make a short list of the things that make you the happiest in your work and your life. Linking happiness to your skill set and what makes you stand out provides an emotional connection to understanding your superpower. This is because of the sense of accomplishment you get from using your strong skills. It's a powerful thing when you are good at something and doing it makes you happy.
4. Write down three stories that connect to those turning points in your life when you realized you were special. What were those special moments? What happened to make you feel good? What did you accomplish? How were you strong? They could happen at any time during your life, and they likely built on one another to get you to where you are today.
5. Think about all of this and *create your superpower*. Those moments will help you see, believe, and understand that your happiness, combined with the skills and success that make you stand out, is a ladder up to the true superpower

that you possess. The deeper your understanding of this superpower, the more opportunity you will find to use it for your benefit and the benefit of others.

Not everyone is good at everything. As a matter of fact, *no one* is good at everything. Thankfully, being very good at very few things creates a high level of competency that can be leveraged to get to CEO.

QUICK COACHING SESSION:

1. Using the criteria above, what is your superpower?

___

2. How can you use it to achieve more success?

___

3. How can you use it to create more win-win situations for yourself and others?

___

CHAPTER 4

What Does Success Mean to You?

Success is not the result of spontaneous combustion. You must set yourself on fire.

—ARNOLD H. GLASOW

Success means taking action. To underscore the quote above: "Set yourself on fire." Depending on your goals, this can look like losing weight, getting promoted, finding the right spouse, getting pregnant, winning the game tonight, winning the big account, or any number of minor or major victories.

The key is understanding what success means to you. As a result, you can narrow your focus for faster growth. Part of the premise of this book is for me to share some of the strategies I've used over the years to achieve what I have achieved. I also want to be clear that I have stumbled and been humbled many times. I hope sharing those mistakes and mishaps will help you avoid them.

So, let's get down to being specific about what success means to you. Focusing on what makes you feel successful will increase your growth speed and will bring to the surface the things that are most important for you to be spending your time and effort on.

Clearly, these things that bring you a true sense of success should be integrated into how you think about setting goals and your strategies for achieving them.

So, make a list of ten things you do that make you feel a true sense of success. This sense of success could be excitement, energy, or pride. It is a feeling of motivation and the belief that you can achieve it again.

This could also be a much longer list! The key is that you feel successful when you do these things. Once you have this list, rank the items. Prioritize each and assign a rating from one to ten, so you can determine how each makes you feel in terms of achievement.

Once you have created and rearranged your list, take it all in. Relive those moments. Feel the emotions you have from these successes. Think back to how you got there and the skills that brought you there. After you have had a chance to catch up with yourself and be in the moment, write a paragraph on what each success *means* to you. How did it make you feel? How did it affect others around you? How does it enhance your self-worth, confidence, and ability to get up in the morning? How does it foster belief in your spiritual self or bolster what is necessary to make you successful today?

Describe what that success truly means to you.

Success to one particular CEO meant helping his overwrought, sobbing mother pay the rent.

A close friend— let's call him Lance, the CEO of a global business—then eight years old, sat at the kitchen table while his mom paid the bills. She worked as a teacher, and making ends meet did not come easy. An alcoholic husband and father, who had left them years earlier, further complicated things. Lance sat distraught while his mom cried and peeled checks off her thin checkbook. She knew when she completed the task, there would be no money left for food.

Lance agonized over his mom's distress. He loved her and could see that she suffered greatly knowing she wasn't able to properly take care of them.

What did success mean for Lance?

"I'm gonna make some money, so I can give it to my mom," he promised himself.

Can an eight-year-old make enough to help with the rent? To earn extra money, Lance typically turned in glass bottles for a few cents. He figured that would be the best way to help his mom—but he needed lots of bottles.

At first, he started going dumpster diving after school. Soon, though, he approached the fraternity houses in the college town where he lived to convince the students that letting him take their bottles would reduce their garbage pick-up costs.

It worked.

His business thrived, and he helped his mom. But things still weren't that easy. He recalls living in twenty different places before his tenth birthday. They stayed in rentals as long as they could and then slept in their car for a few days until they found the next place.

"An overwhelming sense of need drove me," he told me. "It was all about effort. I guess at some point I decided that I was going to be the hardest working guy ever. It pushed me for a long time as a source of motivation to avoid what my mom and I suffered."

He did all this to help his mom.

Those success moments that he developed drove not only his work ethic, but his long-term vision to be successful by always pushing. He recalled, "I guess at thirty years old, I looked back and recognized I had some success. I thought, 'Wow, this is what life looks like when you don't have to look over your shoulder all the time.'"

Although Lance continues to build his successful business, using those same success moments to give him the confidence to keep going, he still looks over his shoulder—but this time for different things. He looks for people in the same situation he suffered through and supports them. He supports his employees, community, and others who require a helping hand to get back on track.

Success moments of all kinds drive belief, work ethic, confidence, and a better future.

Understand yours and how they drive your success.

QUICK COACHING SESSION:

1. List ten things you do that make you feel a true sense of success.

   _____
   _____
   _____
   _____
   _____
   _____
   _____

2. Close your eyes and relive moments of each of those successes. Internalize them.

   _____
   _____
   _____
   _____
   _____
   _____
   _____

3. Write a paragraph on what success means to you.

   _____
   _____
   _____
   _____
   _____
   _____
   _____

CHAPTER 5

What Drives Your Success?

Success is most often achieved by those who don't know that failure is inevitable.

—COCO CHANEL

Understanding your successful moments is the first step toward driving even more success.

The drivers or elements of your success are embedded in those moments. Think about and deconstruct them—recognizing and internalizing what makes you good and drives your success can lead you to create more. What were you so good at that created that moment?

A particular skill?
The way you treated someone?
Your perseverance?
Specialized knowledge?

Let's drill down even more. What is your single biggest success driver in the last three months? This can be the driver of a big success you achieved, or the magic behind several small but notable successes. This could be driving more opportunity for your work, helping your children, finding a mate, or what got you promoted. What are the positive impacts it has made for you?

Now, how can you throw gas on that fire to enhance it? Through understanding those drivers, we want to make you better at what you're already good at.

Throwing gas on a fire to show off his success drivers is exactly what Mark Springer, CEO of Dayspring Restoration, did. His restoration company provides all the services necessary to restore homes or offices to their original state following a devastating fire, flood, or other natural disaster.

Mark took over this small business from his father and felt highly motivated to grow it. He had already invested substantially in training and development for his people, far beyond what other restoration companies had done. He had worked in the business since childhood, vacuuming wet carpets, hauling trash, and carrying out the destroyed belongings of those who had suffered a disaster.

He studied the business, analyzed it, understood it, lived it, and had a great passion for it. Now that he was at the helm, he wanted to take that fire and turn it into massive growth for Dayspring.

How could he demonstrate the skills and value his team could bring to folks in need when disaster hits? Few people even understand what a restoration company does.

That's where he saw an opportunity.

He didn't just run to the fire; he decided to take bold steps to *create* a fire. Mark concocted a scheme where he started a fire in his own kitchen (after, of course, he cleared the idea with his wife). They watched as everything became engulfed in flames and destroyed the kitchen—all while they filmed it for Dayspring TV commercials!

He did the same thing with a flood. For the purposes of another highly effective advertising campaign, he flooded his own home, on purpose. What better way to demonstrate the capability of his restoration business than to burn and flood his own house, then restore it before the eyes of his potential customers in an advertising campaign?

Mark's clear entrepreneurial approach—to do what others are not willing to do—created great success. His business grew substantially, he expanded offices, and he became the most well-known restoration company in the state. This is the epitome of running to and lighting the fire!

Having spent my entire life in the advertising business, searching constantly for big, enduring, business-building ideas for my clients, I loved watching Mark star in his own ads, most of which are still on YouTube. All are conceived, written, and created by the CEO.

Mark has an entrepreneurial fire. He bet his house on it.

Everyone has different success drivers and superpowers, and sharing these with others helps all of us to learn. It gives us different blueprints that might work for us. Those who work with you or are around you will appreciate you sharing that knowledge with them—and vice versa. This isn't a teacher/learner exercise. This is an opportunity for you to speak humbly about what you have achieved, including your stumbles and fumbles, and what you learned in the process of building your success.

Part of the routine of success is recounting and rehashing your victories: What am I doing right? Do more opportunities like this exist? What success elements did I learn that I can repeat? How do I achieve the same great results the next time?

People often force themselves to rehash only their screwups and end up languishing in dread or self-pity. Though understanding mistakes is necessary for learning, if you force yourself to analyze only your negative results and effort, getting motivated is awfully tough.

My struggle and learning process started there.

I often felt so badly about making mistakes that I spent most of my time trying to understand where my actions, judgement, or leadership failed. Although I suffered an arduous process, I learned a lot. But I dreaded it.

I would break down my process into simple steps and then come up with "Lessons Learned." I borrowed the "Lessons Learned" idea from the essential work I performed for clients. We would analyze prior marketing or advertising campaigns and communicate to our clients the lessons we learned and what we could enhance in new creative development or marketing programming. This wasn't taught to me in business school. It got drummed into my head on the job. It became part of my problem evaluation mindset.

I simply adapted that thinking to myself. Unfortunately, in the same way I performed the work for my clients, I tended to focus on mistakes I had made, what didn't work, and where I hadn't succeeded.

I ran that process until a seminal moment with a mentor of mine. We were celebrating a "victory," discussing the story of how a new client meeting was successful and we won a major account. Though this multinational assignment had been a substantial team effort, I had led the charge. While I told this story, my mentor was totally engaged in the narrative and excited about my success. Then he got a knowing smile on his face.

"So, what did you learn from the process of winning that business?" he intoned quizzically.

I sat there dumbfounded.

Until now, I had never thought about deconstructing a good experience. I simply felt buoyed by the confidence from it and continued to do things in the way I found success. But my mentor made me think about the elements that were the biggest difference makers: how we put the team together, how we illustrated our thinking, who presented, how we arrived at the data, and which prospective clients were present. Recognizing and thinking through what created this victory helped me break down and understand its success factors—which meant we could adopt those elements in the future.

Going through the good stuff—great work, a job you received accolades for, positive peer or client feedback—is vital. Understanding what made it good reinforces your work routines, focus, positive actions, knowledge of the subject matter, and effective team dynamics.

Finding little achievements in your mistakes is as necessary as learning from outright success. Establishing your routine of analyzing what you are doing well, in all contexts, will bring great confidence and belief that *you can do it again.*

Build confidence from within. Recognize your growth moments—moments where, despite success or failure, you learned something you didn't already know.

Understand and internalize that your growth builds confidence.

Confidence helps you fight off fear and release risk. The less you are worried about risk, the easier it is to believe.

Belief is a powerful tool for success.

QUICK COACHING SESSION:

1. Think of three successful moments in your life. Tell yourself the stories of each. What were the key drivers?

_____
_____
_____
_____
_____
_____
_____

2. How did they build your unique strengths?

_____
_____
_____
_____
_____
_____
_____

3. Think of three stories that you can share with others so that they can also benefit from your learning.

_____
_____
_____
_____
_____
_____
_____

CHAPTER 6

How Do You Influence Others?

They may forget what you said—but they will never forget how you made them feel.

—CARL W. BUEHNER

Whether you know it or not, when you walk into a room, people observe your every move.

Part of being self-aware is understanding how you influence others. A simple way to imagine this is when you enter a room. Some people in the room may know you; some may not. How you hold yourself, how you speak, how you act, and how you look are all part of who you are. Everything is on parade when you enter a room. Each of these dictates whether you will be listened to, understood, feared, or disregarded.

Being self-aware of how you make an entrance is important. This became obvious to me once when I walked into a room to meet a new colleague and she said, "Wow! You're a big guy!"

As she stepped back and regarded me, I thought, *Well yes, I've played basketball. I'm six foot six.* Height had always created positive vibes and confidence in my life so far. In this moment, however, I somewhat shocked her. She stood five foot two, was whip-smart, and introduced herself as my new boss.

As it turned out, we became good colleagues and friends—but in that moment my size had been turned around on me. I did not want to intimidate anyone, much less my boss. I had never experienced the negative aspect of being tall. So, I started to do some simple things. I tended to be the last one that walked into a room with a group of people, and I began to slouch down a little bit so I would be on the same physical level as others during conversation. Although it sometimes bothered me that I had to do that, I found it to be a good people-connecting strategy.

To be humbly confident, rather than intimidating, I needed to be cognizant of my size and natural self-assurance with those who didn't know me.

Your smarts, success, and persona when you enter a room—known or unknown—is important.

Recognizing who you are and how you operate in front of people is an important part of gaining self-awareness. They will play a key role in helping you build relationships faster.

Get feedback from others about what it was like to meet you. What won them over? How did they begin to trust you? Did their initial perception of you change? Why? Analyze their answers and use the feedback to modify how you interact with those you don't know, so you can build rapport with them quicker.

Ray Dalio, founder and co-chief investment officer of Bridgewater Associates, is one of the most successful hedge fund managers of all time. His book, *Principles*, describes how he took his success drivers and turned them into influential concepts to help his employees. He didn't want to be the guru. He didn't want to be the one with all the answers. He didn't want people to be afraid of him and tremble when he walked into a room. He wanted to empower them with the knowledge he had learned about how to be successful in business. He wanted to give them the tools to create at the same level he had learned to create. He wanted to positively influence his people by helping them understand and use the success drivers that fueled him.

You can walk into a room in different ways. Be recognized as someone who can help, create opportunity, and positively influence others. Be self-aware, and remember that as a leader, people will judge you as a giver or a taker.

Become the giver.

QUICK COACHING SESSION:

1. What is your assessment of how people view you?

2. Is it different if they know you?

3. What do you need to change to make the answers to the above questions more equivalent?

PART TWO

PERFORMANCE ROUTINE

What Is Performance?

Am I thinking new thoughts right now that will enhance who I am today? Am I destined to perform better today than yesterday?

Performance is in the eye of the beholder. Is it you against you? Is it you against someone else? Is it you against some vision of what you expect yourself to be? This is a question *you* need to answer. I don't believe you should chase specters—the real performance question is in your own mind. Am I better than yesterday's performance? Am I better this month than last month? Am I better this year than last year?

Performance is about productivity, but you don't get productivity or achieve any kind of success without the right mindset and an understanding of what you're trying to achieve. Think of yourself like an athlete. Athletes train tirelessly, and must continuously improve and recognize that their competition is doing the same thing. That drives them. They believe they can achieve specific success no matter the field of play. They understand their responsibility to themselves, to their team, and to their fans. They understand what it means for their families.

Performance is personal, but it's also a community and team sport.

Part two of the book helps you to develop the routines, mindsets, measurement techniques, and learning strategies to perform at the highest level you can.

CHAPTER 7

What Is Your Signature?

Create and maintain a compelling signature: It's influence with purpose.
—CURTIS BRACKENBURY OF NHL'S EDMONTON OILERS.

When your performance matters to your team, identifying your signature is important. I learned this concept from my dear friend, Curtis Brackenbury. Curtis is an ex-NHL player, pro sailor, and a performance coach. He's a brilliant self-taught man who can speak as fluently about neurobiology as he can about how a hockey player needs to have their head on a swivel and the edge of their skates in the right direction when they go into a corner to avoid a body check.

Curtis and I spent many hours together in what was a veritable tutorial for me to learn the high-performance methods he used to coach my hockey-playing sons. He also helped my daughters who were elite horseback riders.

During our chat, Curtis often spoke of the "signature." To understand your signature, you'll have to ask some questions:

What do you want to be known for? What are you preparing yourself for? How will your competition perceive you? What skills do you need to develop so that you can achieve the level you want to achieve?

The signature is as unique as your own handwriting. It's your brand. It's your character. It's the residue that you leave when you have influenced someone. It's the thing that makes you the most recognizable. Are you a hard worker? Do you go above and beyond? Are you always taking initiative? Are you a problem solver? Are you an ideas person? Are you a great executor? Are you a great strategist? Are you a deep thinker who can also communicate and execute plans flawlessly?

Knowing how you want to show up is as important as making sure you have the requisite skills.

Once you figure out your signature, get in the game and stay there. Be consistent. Believe in your abilities. Grow your abilities. Develop a learning plan that will help you enhance your signature. You, your family, your team, and your career will all benefit from this work, as each depends upon your performance.

A big part of building your confidence and your signature is to develop a performance plan. Here are a few ways to do that:

- Plan meticulously, daily and weekly.
- Set priorities clearly.
- Monitor performance constantly.

- Clearly lay out your priorities and tasks around your personal life and career.
- Prioritize ruthlessly.

What is the most important must-do? Identify this every day, every hour, every minute—whether it's tough to do or not. Even if you are unmotivated to do it, think it through and act. Can you delegate it? Do you really need to do it? Is it really that important? Will it move the needle?

Focus on your strong suits and build your confidence. Your skills should move your personal and professional needle. Make sure you use them. If those high priorities and powerful skills are not being used, then you are missing the opportunity to achieve your greatest goals. What can you stop doing or delegate out that would allow you to focus more intensely on those great strengths and top priorities?

Always remember that your signature may change over time, depending upon your growth and the roles you take on. Although you will always have your basic strengths, continual growth is important and enhancing your signature is paramount.

Early in my career I amassed a fair amount of management experience for a young leader. I had the opportunity to work in four countries in leadership positions, both running major accounts as well as leading offices in Europe and North America. I recall meeting a major client soon after I transferred to Canada, and he asked me about my experience. I went through my résumé, highlighting the things that I thought he might like to know or that would benefit him and his needs. I proudly included foreign languages I spoke, countries I had worked in, and global clients I had experience with.

And then he asked a question that I didn't expect.

"Can you golf?"

He went on to talk a bit more about golfing before he made me answer the question. Unfortunately, I didn't play golf then, and I still don't play very well now. But clearly my client partner loved playing golf, and I needed to play with him.

Unfortunately, golf was not part of my signature! I had a young family and—having moved five times in eight years to different countries for work—golf had not yet made it onto the calendar. Although I learned to play as a kid, my skills were greatly diminished.

Golf, as a part of my relationship-building signature, had suddenly become important. I started getting up at five each morning so I could make a six o'clock golf lesson five days a week. This diligence helped me up my game with my client, though I never really felt like I played on par with him. I considered dedicating myself to building on and expanding my signature to be a great achievement, but that still didn't stop him from giving me annoying lessons on the course.

A couple years later, a headhunter contacted me to throw my hat in the ring to become the president of a much larger organization. The last round of interviews took place in New York, and as I fidgeted in the executive waiting room,

I glanced at a stack of magazines; I needed a distraction. A trade magazine lay innocently on the coffee table. The front-page story—an exposé on the person who had just been fired from the role I intended to get hired for—shocked me. I went quickly from needing a distraction to reading the article with some zest, thinking that I might gain insight into the company's important issues and what they were looking for in a new leader.

When they called my name, I felt pretty good. Armed with confidence and a bit of new information, I walked in, shook hands, and sat down. The interviewer—a courtly, congenial guy—engaged straight away in conversation… about art. Art? In the communications and advertising business, the art we produced sold things. We rarely dealt with art for art's sake. My wife is a brilliant art historian and has studied all the greats. Unfortunately, she did not accompany me into the interview to whisper in my ear.

Sue and I had relished walking through the art museums in Europe. We often spent time in galleries and occasionally bought some local art in the countries in which we were fortunate to live. But, when it came to the classics, I didn't retain much information.

Interestingly, my lack of art knowledge is all I can remember about the interview. Although I can recall feigning some pseudo art sophistication, I clearly could not foster an intelligent conversation about fine art. Although I had several interviews with other executives, it's all a blur. I don't even think I got an opportunity to use the information I'd culled from the magazine article.

Looking back over it now, I'm sure it may have been some kind of test—one that I clearly failed because I didn't get the job. It didn't fit my signature. I'm sure I would have been successful in the job I interviewed for; I had all the skills and experience required.

But often that doesn't matter.

Many people have all the skills required to do the work. But you also need to fit the culture and understand who you're dealing with if you want to get the job. They were looking for a certain type of individual, and I wasn't that person.

Not every role is right for you. Clearly this one did not fit me, but deconstructing it and learning from it is good. You must understand how your signature needs to be enhanced, the skills you need to learn, the knowledge you need to retain, and—as you mature—the growth that you need to succeed.

QUICK COACHING SESSION:

1. What is your signature?

   _____
   _____
   _____
   _____
   _____
   _____
   _____
   _____

2. What skills do you need to enhance to make sure your signature is unique and strong?

   _____
   _____
   _____
   _____
   _____
   _____
   _____
   _____

3. What strengths can you build on so that they become big confidence builders for you as you grow and mature?

   _____
   _____
   _____
   _____
   _____
   _____
   _____
   _____

CHAPTER 8

Establish Highly Productive Routines

Amateurs sit and wait for inspiration; the rest of us just get up and go to work.
—CHUCK CLOSE

To some, this chapter title may seem like a bit of a joke. Routines are often given a bad rap. They are boring. They are the throwaway parts of the day and potentially the least exciting. A routine is what you do when you don't know what to do. Right?

So, why does poet W. H. Auden say, "Routine, in an intelligent man, is a sign of ambition"?

Although the word "routine" connotes ordinariness or even being on autopilot and not thinking, having set daily rituals saves time that you can then devote to being wildly creative. A daily routine is really a personal choice, and when linked together with other simple routines, it creates the opportunity for you to be more disciplined and develop superior willpower to accomplish your toughest and most creative tasks.

Good routines help you form good habits, and they eliminate negotiating with yourself. Negotiating with yourself is the biggest procrastination problem that humans face. It's the reason why many stop going to the gym or push away big problems because they don't want to deal with them. But if you have a routine where dealing with those kinds of issues is a normal part of your day, you won't overlook them. You will waltz through them with your regular focus and effort, and not allow them to slow you down.

The place to start with highly productive routines is the morning.

The morning is the beginning of your day. It sets the pace for learning, achieving, thinking, and problem solving. It's the best part of the day for the mind.

The masters of our time use it to their greatest benefit. Stephen King rises daily at six o'clock, begins writing before eight o'clock, and does not get up from his writing table until he has completed two thousand words. He does this every day of the year, all 365 days. He does it on Christmas, his birthday, and holidays. He has developed this routine and does not allow himself to stray from it. No writer's block at Stephen King's writing table. He simply does not allow it to happen (King 2000).

Kobe Bryant, one of the world's greatest basketball players, rose daily at four o'clock to take shooting practice and develop his skills, prior to team practice starting six hours later at ten o'clock. He would finish the team practice and stay hours afterward to shoot jump shots or free throws to complete his workout.

Imagine working out at 100 percent for six hours prior to your regular team practice. While on the road, the team would arrive at their destination the day before the game. Kobe would often have the driver drop him at a prearranged practice gym as late as midnight, so he could practice the night before a game (Sielsky 2022). It's no wonder Kobe could walk through other teams and beat even super-elite players with ease.

This kind of preparation might seem unusual for normal folk. But for the masters, it's the norm.

If we go back into the 1700s, we can see that Wolfgang Mozart arose daily at six in the morning, had his hair finished, and began to compose for two hours. Following composing, he taught lessons for three hours and then went back to his composing for another three hours (Currey 2013).

The simple routine of doing what they did every day is what created the elite performance of these individuals. Practice. Practice. Practice. No negotiating with yourself. And once you get into the groove of a routine, as these masters did, you are on autopilot—and that autopilot is developing an elite level within you. Muscle memory is a beautiful thing.

The biggest part of establishing a highly productive routine is how it eliminates decision fatigue. Go back over all the videos you've ever seen of Steve Jobs, and you will never see him without a black turtleneck. Jobs wore a black turtleneck every day as a routine, so that he wouldn't have to spend decision time on what to wear. The more decisions you make as a part of the day, the more your brain gets fatigued. And as your brain fatigues, decision quality goes down.

Some of these masters, including Jobs, essentially became radical "routine-izers" who created multiple routines per day they dutifully followed so that the mundane bits of life were on autopilot. Their minds were free and unencumbered by unimportant matters so that precious creative time could be used to solve much more important problems.

As a last (and maybe most important) example, Benjamin Franklin also established a very simple routine. Every day he arose at five in the morning and asked himself one question: What good shall I do today? In the evening as he climbed into bed, he asked himself the evening question: What good have I done today? (Currey 2013).

Beginning your routines with intention helps you spend proper time on your goals, enhancing the thought process necessary to achieve at the highest level. Routines condition the "great muscle" of your mind to drive yourself to excellence.

Routines are far from boring.

That said, I struggled with them. I found that with a large family and a demanding leadership job, finding time to think, develop myself, settle my anxieties, or stay in shape became impossible.

To address this, I read and listened to Tony Robbins, Grant Cardone, and Tim Ferriss on developmental work for solid morning routines. I believe Robin Sharma has developed exceptional work in his book, *The 5AM Club*, to bring spirit, knowledge, and vitality to learning about the value of a great morning routine. I found that Sharma's simple program, with a few modifications, worked best for me. It gave me many real reasons to get up at five in the morning and greatly enhanced my productivity and confidence. I also learned that highly successful people practice this skill as a part of their performance success.

Having studied and tried several morning routines, here is what works for me. I hope it may serve you.

1. THE "GET UP."
Get up early, between four thirty and six in the morning. Beat the sun. This gets you going before 98 percent of humans on the planet. It builds confidence and creates a positive mindset that you are conquering opportunity before anyone else is out of bed.

2. THE "GET GOING."
Now it's time to build your mind, body, and spirit before you start doing any work. Let's call this "the power ninety." It has three simple parts:

PART 1.

Work your body with a thirty-minute workout of some kind. Break a sweat. Push some weight around. Do some yoga. Stretch. Don't negotiate with yourself. Just do it. That's the first thirty minutes.

PART 2.

Feed your spirit. During the second thirty minutes, write in a journal. Meditate. Calm yourself. Keep your mind open and available.

PART 3.

Feed your mind. In the last thirty minutes, spend some time learning. Listen to a podcast. Read a book. Watch a video of someone who is very good at a skill that you would like to acquire. This is time is for growth and learning. It is not intended to pass the time with fiction reading.

Doing the power ninety every morning will launch you into a stronger body, a calmer mind, and a spirit you have not known before.

Imagine the compound effect of thirty minutes of workout, journaling, and learning. Each day, every day. Body. Spirit. Mind.

Now for those who don't have ninety minutes that early in the morning, I recommend a power thirty. The key thing is that you build a routine. It almost doesn't matter how long it is because you can adjust for your time. The most important thing is to feed your body with some exercise, your spirit with a journal and meditation, your mind with some learning. Ten minutes each is all you need.

The main thrust here is that you do it daily and build the habit.

Now, maybe it goes without saying, but I am going to say it anyway: all this personal development must be performed without your phone or any kind of notifications, emails, texts, feed checking, or disruptions.

You need a clean environment. Find a place where you are uninterrupted. You must not engage with low priority tasks. Completely eliminate all notifications on your phone. If you need your phone to listen to a podcast or watch an educational video, make sure you have killed all notifications. Don't do anything that could divert your attention.

Now you can start your life's best work. And every single day is the first day of your life's best work.

Design your day. Design your life. Be meticulous and relentless by paying lots of attention to how you plan your time and what you allow into that time. Prioritize your biggest issues and life goals.

Having read hundreds of books on productivity and listened to many productivity experts who are knowledgeable about the human brain's ability to concentrate, I find the following to be the most productive methods for me:

1. Meticulously go over your daily plan and ask yourself, "What's the most important needle-moving project I have today?"

You have just taken a major step toward simplifying your life and your focus. That's the first thing you do. You then ask yourself what comes in second and what comes in third. Be specific and design your day with concentration and world-class production in mind.

You might be thinking about how to be a better parent or how to complete a tough project at work or how to find your way through a difficult day. You can't do any of these things at a high level without focus. Identifying the real reasons behind your biggest needle-moving project every day will provide insight into solving it. But you will not solve it without complete focus.

2. With complete focus, work on that top needle-moving project until it's finished. I call this the "one 'til done" rule. Simply work on that top priority, first thing each day, until it's done. Then you move to the next one.

This assures that your top priority gets done first and you have supported it with your most creative thinking and your freshest mind.

3. Work in focus periods. I call this "seventy-five focus." Work for seventy-five minutes and take a fifteen-minute break. Go get a coffee. Do some deep breathing. Go for a walk in the woods. Go for a walk around the block. Do something that frees your mind and allows the

endorphins to rush back in so that you can take on the next seventy-five minutes and solve your biggest problems with complete concentration. If necessary, set a clock to stay on this cycle. You need the recovery as much as you need the focused work.
4. Remember that you are focused on your daily top three priorities that will move the needle in your life and in your work.

Remember to avoid small unnecessary tasks or small bits that don't move the needle, and don't let your mind wander to unproductive places. Avoid being busy *being busy*. Constantly reevaluate this work you're doing. Will this move an important needle in my life or work forward?

5. Clean up. Once you have nailed a very productive three hours' worth of work, it's time to do some cleanup. These are the administrative tasks that everyone has and simply needs to do. Go through your emails. Return important texts. Return important voicemails. If social media is a part of your work, go ahead and post or monitor your feeds. Stay focused on doing important work. Clean up the daily tasks of staying connected, and make sure your colleagues are kept in the loop on your work. The same applies with your family.

Only perform these cleanup tasks after you have nailed your top priority that day. Plan the rest of your day with thoughtfulness and open mindedness as to what your prioritized work still requires.

Although this direction is focusing on your work and personal routine, make sure that your family or friends play an important role in your priorities. Balancing your family and work can be a great challenge, and it takes time, effort, and commitment to get it right. It's one of the most important parts of your life—and your work.

6. Lastly, as your day winds down, be grateful for it! Think about your strengths, abilities, and gains. Acknowledge and be grateful for your wins. Think about how you helped others—including your family, friends, and colleagues. Then think about who helped *you*.

Think about how the love of service and the love for yourself has been enhanced with all the learning and achievement in this day.

Great routines enhance your life!

QUICK COACHING SESSION:

1. What are your best routines?

2. What routines can you start to become ten times more productive?

3. Do a start, stop, continue exercise. List all the tasks you do each day and decide if they are important enough to continue in your routine. If you have tasks to do, start doing them. If tasks don't serve you or your needle-moving mission, either rid them from your life or delegate them to someone else.

CHAPTER 9

Learn and Don't Stop Learning

As I grow older, I pay less attention to what men say; I just watch what they do.

—ANDREW CARNEGIE

If you ask people in today's workforce, they might say their best training came from on-the-job experience. Obviously, working the job and learning its ins and outs as well as its demands is very important. Doing so provides the cues and the tasks for accomplishment in earning a living. It provides mistakes, victories, new learning from colleagues, and everything else that a day-to-day job brings in terms of experience in one's life.

But simple on-the-job learning only fulfills a small part of getting to success. You also need to prepare for success by trying to understand future needs. Simply said, if you want to keep growing you need to get smart about stuff you don't know. Sometimes that happens on the job—but often it doesn't.

For example, how can you prepare to be a manager of people if you aren't managing anyone? If on-the-job experience is all you have been offered by your employer, and a promotion moves you into a role where you are managing people, how will you prepare?

Believe me, I understand the value of workplace experience. In my first job, I spent fifteen years with the same organization. I started working in the US, got transferred to Germany after four years, stayed there for another four years, then spent three years in Denmark and Sweden. My wife Sue and I went to Europe with no kids. After seven years there, four of our amazing children were born in two different countries. By that time, I had learned two languages and progressed from an account manager to a managing director. I became a vice president in the global company and progressed quickly as a young leader.

I can recall having a conversation with a colleague who had just finished reading a Tom Clancy novel. He loved the way Tom Clancy developed characters, displayed great imagination, and described the political drama. Clancy, a very popular novelist at the time, had sold millions of books, and his name riddled the best-selling book lists for years—but I had never heard of him. I didn't watch TV. I didn't read books.

What had I done instead? Sue and I started a family, learned a couple languages, moved three times in six years, and developed a lot of "experiential learning."

But, I offhandedly thought, *his excitement about this book is so infectious, maybe I'll read it.* It helped that he'd just finished it on a plane and handed me the paperback copy.

I picked up that book and couldn't put it down. It enthralled me and completely dominated my mind every night as I fell asleep reading. I realized at that moment that I hadn't engaged in an entire world of living and learning outside of my own experience. Though I had achieved a lot experientially, much more out there existed—particularly around leadership, business process, and management. My experiences had grown and propelled me forward, career-wise, very quickly. It was my knowledge that needed to catch up.

Now, admittedly, Tom Clancy's novel did not tell a business story or a tale of personal performance or anything that might teach me about stuff I didn't know. But it did open my mind and fully engaged me in a way that I hadn't experienced in a long time. At that point, I started buying books in bookstores as I traveled and began reading voraciously about leadership, management, and how to run a company. I devoured inspirational books designed to enhance me as a leader, a person, and a father.

I also bought every Tom Clancy book ever written...

Now, on-the-job learning is incredible. But off-the-job learning takes additional commitment, time, and effort that is difficult to come by. The most successful people on the planet are voracious readers for a reason.

One needs to commit, learn, and put new practices into play. You need to get on top of a changing world. You need to bombard your mind with new thinking, and you need to pick and choose what can work for you. This is only possible if you are an avid reader, podcast listener, and watcher of documentaries. You also need to learn from others who have already been where you want to go. I'll repeat that: Become a student of people who have made the mistakes and have already learned what you want to know. Follow them.

If you are committed to nonstop learning, you will break all barriers to success and performance. This is a grand advantage that anyone can create for themselves. If you take the steps listed above to keep your body and mind working and keep growing beyond what you learn on the job, you will always be ready to take on the next challenge. And the next challenge could be an uphill one.

A boss and mentor of mine shared this advice early in my career: "Try to be right 51 percent of the time." It is some of the most important guidance I ever received. I try to live by it and have passed it on in hope others might benefit from it. The thought this conveyed to me kickstarted my own personal development and growth process. It made me consciously think about decision making.

I wouldn't have gotten that advice without a mentor offering it to me.

Developing yourself is hard when you are the only one watching. Having a mentor provides a second dimension to your growth and learning curve. We all learn from a lot of people.

Your first mentors are really those in books and podcasts. I have learned from many—Napoleon Hill, Peter Drucker, John Wooden, John Maxwell, Tony Robbins, Dean Graziosi, Marcus Aurelius, Phil Knight, Sam Walton, Robin Sharma, Jim Collins, and Tim Ferris, to name a few. I also cherish Walter Isaacson's books on Steve Jobs, Albert Einstein, and Leonardo da Vinci. Different types of books—autobiographies, biographies, corporate case studies, team building, coaching—can provide insights related to personal growth, leadership, making mistakes, and the knowledge necessities of high performance. These books can provide powerful starts to your mastery of the skills and states of mind necessary to persevere in your own success.

That is step one. Soak it all in. Consider and evaluate the insights; think them through in a journal that you consistently try to keep. Put things into practice that make sense, so you can see and feel yourself growing.

Now, you might be interested in taking the next step: finding a real person to guide you further. A mentor is someone you trust who has been where you want to go and has the sincere inclination to want to help you. This person can be within your company or outside it. It doesn't need to be the CEO. Ideally, it's someone a couple levels ahead of you in their development or title, so they can guide you, help you see around corners, and give you advice that is anchored in lived experience.

They should also be of high moral character and capable of keeping things confidential. Interestingly, you may not know this person right now. If they are more senior or in a different company or business, you will need to network to seek them out. Talk to people. Tell them what you are looking for. Consciously seeking a mentor is a serious show of your interest in growth, learning, and peak performance.

Choose a mentor who exemplifies the kind of leader you want to become and is someone you can learn from.

Here is a good checklist in your search for a mentor. Using the acronym COACH, author John Maxwell outlines what you should look for and what a mentor can do for you:

Care for the people they coach.
Observe their attitudes, behavior, and performance.
Align them with their strengths for peak performance.
Communicate and give feedback about their performance.
Help them to improve their lives and performance.

Finding a mentor is a crucial step to help you improve your life and career.

QUICK COACHING SESSION:

1. How can you commit the time to read a book a month? A book a month is easy! If you simply read thirty minutes a day (that's 182 hours a year) you could easily devour twenty to twenty-five books yearly.

   _____
   _____
   _____
   _____

2. Identify events, virtual or otherwise, that could enhance your skills, learning, networking, and experiences. Can you attend two per year?

   _____
   _____
   _____
   _____

3. What organizations can you join that jibe with your interests? These could be work-related interests, family-related hobbies, health, or simply things that will break your own boundaries.

   _____
   _____
   _____
   _____

4. Who are your mentors? What have you learned from them? Do you need to search one out?

   _____
   _____
   _____

CHAPTER 10

Pause and Reflect

You should sit in meditation for twenty minutes every day—unless you're too busy. Then you should sit for an hour.
—ZEN PROVERB

Scary stuff can sneak up on you.

This is where the choices you make can change your life. Being self-aware, recognizing the moment, and taking the time to pause and reflect on these situations is paramount. Sometimes you need to get slapped in the face to recognize the importance of things.

To illustrate this point, I want to share a pivotal moment in my life where I almost blew it.

We had just moved for the fourth time to our fourth country in seven years. Keeping it together and transitioning to new experiences and cultures meant exciting and constant challenges. I had been very career-driven, and although we moved a lot, we enjoyed the change and the excitement of each new foreign city we lived in. But with the constant upheaval of moving and my work and travel load, stress at home was mounting.

Our growing family—at the time five children under seven years old—demanded a herculean parental effort, even more so in foreign countries with no other family support. I worked hard at being a great dad, but Sue carried most of the parental weight. An incredible mom, she worked hard at home, usually in a new home and new country, with new neighbors and new doctors. Every time we moved, we (she) started from scratch. Sue's resilience made each promotion and move a reality. Without her, I would not have enjoyed the career trajectory I experienced. We are a great team, but life kept getting more complex, and keeping things steady at home got tougher.

It all came to a head on the day of my most crucial off-site presentation to the largest, most demanding client in the company. We had been working on this senior management presentation for months to solve a significant client marketing issue—and I led it.

Sue called, very distraught, just prior to the meeting.

"Are you having an affair?" she asked.

"What? No! Why are you saying that?" I replied, shocked.

"I found this parking ticket in your jacket. I don't know this address. Where is it? Why were you there? What's going on?"

I sat there, stunned.

I couldn't believe she had construed a parking ticket into an affair. But I recognized that given my work schedule and her workload at home, things had escalated emotionally, making nothing unimaginable.

I explained, "Honey, I got that parking ticket at the company event last week. I parked near the museum. I couldn't find a parking spot, so I parked on a side street, in a 'no parking zone,' and got a ticket."

Awkwardly, I added, "I'm so sorry that finding the ticket made you feel this way. There is no affair. There never was, and there never will be. I am so sorry." It was devastating that I had made my wonderful wife feel so shaky about our relationship.

She broke down in tears. We clearly had many family issues: sick kids, relationship shortcomings, and things I had avoided or not addressed. All this had built up and manifested itself in the parking ticket. I felt like such an idiot.

We discussed things for a few more minutes. I mostly tried to tell Sue that we would get through it, and everything would be all right. I meant it, but my words fell on deaf ears.

Mostly mine.

Everything had built to this moment.

I closed the door to my office and let it all come flooding over me. Everything blew by at a million miles an hour. I agonized over the importance of leading this meeting, while recognizing that Sue was suffering. I reflected—quickly. What had I missed? What had I neglected? How did I choose myself over my wife and family? Where did my ego take over, and what were the consequences?

I shook physically for half an hour. I needed to figure this out. The obvious choice was to get through this meeting then go home to take care of my wife. But I quickly realized that I had made a habit of choosing work first. This is the reason my relationship with Sue had deteriorated; she came in second. Although I am unsure whether I had much clarity in the moment, when I paused to let the emotions course through me and finally subside, the right decision became very clear.

I brought my team in and told them they would have to lead the meeting.

I had to go home.

Sue and I still talk about this pivotal moment in our relationship. Thank goodness, while fumbling my way through it, I had the presence of mind to choose my family. I could have continued to screw up badly, and things may have turned out for the worse. I reflect on this often to keep this important feeling close.

To get the most from growth, we need to pause to let it catch up. If we don't, the moment's significance is lost, and the learning from such pivotal moments is gone. It's about being reflective enough to be self-aware when it matters most, when you have much to gain and much to lose.

Some scary, pivotal moments can screw up your life if you don't sit, reflect, and recognize them before making decisions.

Pausing and reflecting is a lot of work because it takes time. We are all very busy, and time is at a premium. In a grand sense, that's exactly why taking this precious time to let growth and emotion catch up is so important. A work-related event like this might seem like a small thing—but reflecting on it has made me a better person.

So… don't just do. Stop. Think. Write. Talk to someone. Visualize. Imagine the outcome. Contemplate the change.

Then do the right thing.

QUICK COACHING SESSION:

1. Where can you create time in your busy week to pause and think about your path and plan?

   _____
   _____
   _____
   _____
   _____
   _____
   _____

2. Are you already aware of situations where things are in the danger zone? What do you need to think about to make them right?

   _____
   _____
   _____
   _____
   _____
   _____
   _____

3. You have experienced a string of successes. You are buoyed by the accolades and pats on the back. What are you missing?

   _____
   _____
   _____
   _____
   _____
   _____
   _____

CHAPTER 11

Don't Be the Smartest Person In the Room

I'm not the smartest fellow in the world, but I can sure pick smart colleagues.

—FRANKLIN D. ROOSEVELT

Being smart makes things easy, and it really feels good. Why else do you do all this learning? Why do you work so hard reading every day, attending events, listening to podcasts, and spending more time on the job, if for no other reason than to be smart? You are expected to be smart to perform in your job and to lead others to perform. People look up to you and want answers. I'm sure your job is dependent upon you solving problems, and you need to be smart to solve them.

All this is very true and mandatory. But are you really that smart?

How do you grow if you are always the go-to person? Who motivates the motivator? Those who lead hold a grand responsibility. How do you get exponential growth?

Find a new room where you are not the smartest person. You've heard the Jim Rohn quote, "You are the average of the five people you spend the most time with." So, how is that going for you? Are you the smartest person in your room? Are others pushing you from a motivational or a knowledge perspective? Are the tasks you undertake and the people you manage pushing you outside of your comfort zone or into new boundaries?

Can you find a room that pushes your boundaries of capability and knowledge and introduces you to new ways of thinking? Most importantly, can you benefit from the experiences of those who have already been there and done that and made the mistakes?

Oddly, because we spend so much time trying to get smart, we fear finding people who are smarter. But you need people to push your boundaries. You can learn from their experiences, victories, and mistakes. This can push your thinking, open new doors for you, and help you go where you've never gone before.

For example, I took a job running a small startup agency. It had failed under previous management and lost money every single day. The office had a myriad of problems—too many people, not enough clients, too much office space, and a thoroughly demotivated crew—a clear turnaround situation. Going into that kind of an organization, everyone is looking at you. You need to be the person with the plan. I needed to fix things, change things, motivate the troops, build the clients, and make it all work in record time.

I needed to be one of the smart people in the room. The question was: Who makes *me* smarter? The day I accepted the job, I'd thought I knew everything. Then, around three days in, I realized that I had been completely oblivious.

I still marvel at my clueless confidence.

Luckily, after a few months working to turn the company around, a colleague approached me from another company and asked me if I had heard of the Young Presidents' Organization. YPO is a global group of CEOs from businesses ranging widely from small to massive. It's a well-run organization that focuses on personal, family, and business growth. In short order, it became a lifesaver for me. From then on, I met with a group of CEOs in my YPO forum monthly. Eight CEOs sat in the same room going through a very strict and regimented format to elicit help from what turned out to be our own personal board of directors.

These leaders came from all walks of life and all walks of business. They were comprised of entrepreneurs, professional managers, and owners of family businesses. Each came to the room with a semitruck full of experiences, successes, and failures. This roomful of smart people scared me. I worried about admitting my mistakes, worried about admitting what I didn't know, and feared talking about issues related to my business. As a professional manager, I solved problems; I didn't talk about them with people outside the company.

The statement, "It's lonely at the top," is true. It certainly is lonely there. I learned that every single one of the people in that room said they'd felt lonely like I did and had the same fears I had. So, we had each other. Everything got aired in that room: business problems, problems with subordinates, family issues, personal issues—all of it under a strict code of confidentiality.

All meetings were 100 percent confidential. This created an amazing environment for sharing and problem-solving. And most importantly, it solved the problem of being the smartest person in the room. Clearly, I did not wear that mantle, and what a joy! What a learning experience it has turned out to be. I joined that organization over twenty years ago and remain an active member today. I believe it is the single most important business decision I ever made.

Never be the smartest person in the room. If you are, find a new room.

Although organizations like YPO can be transformative in terms of learning, I've learned another way that many claim have changed their lives.

Make a list.

Make a list of thirty people who know a lot more than you about a topic that's important to you. You don't need to know these people right now. In fact, it's probably best if you don't. That means you will need to stretch, be afraid, and push past the "they will never talk to me" feeling.

Remember this point as you're making a list of people who could be great assets to your learning and in your life. You are not simply putting names on a page. Don't be afraid, and don't shy away from making a grand list of people who can guide you with your family, your personal growth, or your business growth. This will help you get out of your comfort zone and network.

Your network is immensely valuable. If you don't have one, you are missing a trick.

How do you reach these people? Use email, social media, LinkedIn, and personal connections to other people you may know. All you're doing is writing an email or a direct message! You would be surprised how many people might be interested in chatting with you to tell their story. That's all you want in this connectivity and networking. You simply want to learn from them and have them tell their story.

You never know where this will go or what you will gain from it. But I guarantee you, you will be smarter coming out of each conversation. Tell your story and have them tell theirs. They will connect with you, and they will want to help. This is a massive opportunity for you.

Lastly and potentially most importantly, find a coach.

A coach's sole role it is to make you the best you can possibly be. They are dedicated, open minded, nonjudgmental, and completely focused on your needs. They are focused on no one else, just you. That dedication comes at a price, though: growth and accountability. You must grow and be dedicated to growth, or the coach will not stick with you. They will hold you accountable every day of the year for agreements you make together to learn, grow, take steps in your business, take steps in your personal life, and achieve. That's their job—maximizing your achievement.

A great coach will not tell you what to do. A great coach will ask you questions so that you figure out and understand what you need to do. They will then keep you accountable in that game. A great coach is simultaneously your personal soldier, your confidante, and your leader. They search for and find the best in you. And they are worth every penny you pay them.

A good coach offers a massive return on investment. They will help you get to places you could never get to on your own because their constant questioning and your constant learning keeps your mind fresh, moving, and growing. They will bring opportunities to you simply by probing into your activities to ask questions that you would never ask yourself.

They will question your business decisions as well as your personal decisions—not to judge them, but to make sure you know what you are doing, why you are doing it, and to assure you are getting a return on your thinking.

To enhance your growth and be challenged, you need to interact with people who are more experienced, more successful, and think differently and bigger than you.

QUICK COACHING SESSION:

1. Make a list of thirty people you could connect with in order to learn a lot more than you currently know about topics that are important to you.

2. Find an organization of people who can fuel you by making sure you are not the smartest person in the room.

3. Act on numbers one and two above.

CHAPTER 12

Measure Your Performance

Measure what is measurable and make measurable what is not so.

—THOMAS-HENRI MARTIN IN
DESCRIBING GALILEO'S METHOD

Performance evaluations—everybody hates them. Within these reviews are moments of weird, uncomfortable conversation with your boss or subordinates. During them, you might think, *Do I really need to set goals and measure them? Do I really need to look myself in the mirror?*

Well, guess what? The short answer is you bet you do. You are constantly being assessed and evaluated by others. Each time you open your mouth, or walk into a room, you are being judged and evaluated—whether they work for you, are unassociated with you, or you work for them.

Why be surprised?

Do you understand your goals and how you are being assessed? You are being measured, so you may as well know what you are being measured for.

Are others' goals the same as yours? Personal? Family? Professional?

Some may be, but not all. When I moved to Canada, having just spent seven years in Europe in a variety of ascending roles, I took over the leadership and management of the agency's largest, most high-profile client account. Inspiring top-notch work, building a trusting client relationship, and fostering teamwork in our agency were crucial to the job.

The chief marketing officer, a sophisticated marketer fifteen years my senior, became my key client. He had managed huge marketing budgets for well-known brands in his career and had found success. I looked forward to learning from and working with him. He also had his own style—smart and a bit old-school.

By this time, I had performed multiple business turnarounds in international offices where I had come in and fixed poor client relationships and unprofitable operations, and had cut my teeth on several of the largest packaged-goods marketing organizations in the world. I came to Canada at a very senior level and took over this slightly troublesome client in a complex business. My confidence soared.

Soon after I arrived, I went to meet with this head client in his office. As we sat down and made a bit of chit-chat, I began to feel uncomfortable—he seemed agitated. I didn't really know him well, so I wanted to try to uncover the source of his uneasiness. I needed to start off strong and build a good relationship.

Somewhat timidly, I asked him, "What's wrong, Mark?"

His response took me by surprise.

He looked down at the desk. It seemed that he didn't want to speak, but then he begrudgingly blurted out the reason for his discontent:

"I am uncomfortable because I am in a suit, and you are wearing jeans and a button-down shirt. I might be old-school, but I don't feel like you show me appropriate respect with your attire. I feel like you should be wearing a coat and tie."

I swallowed hard, somewhat embarrassed and in disbelief. Why would he care about my button-down shirt and jeans?

He continued, "I am also upset that you haven't asked me to dinner with our spouses, so we can get to know each other."

This also took me by surprise. In my European experience, most clients wanted to be home with their families. They weren't interested in purely social relationship events. But, clearly, Mark felt this to be important. His kids were grown, he ran a high-profile business, and he and his wife enjoyed being entertained.

My situation couldn't have been more different. I had five small children, and Sue and I had very little time to go out to dinner for any other purpose than to recover from being overwhelmed by parenting.

"Lastly," he stated with some resentment, "I like to play golf, and if you had done your research on me, you would know that we should be playing golf regularly. You haven't asked me to play golf. We can do a lot of business on the golf course."

What?

I didn't know what to say but bumbled out something like, "Mark, I appreciate you being honest with your feelings. I apologize that my actions (or lack thereof) have created this situation, and I will get my act together."

I also assured him that I would love to have our families dine together. Though I had never played business golf in my life, I surmised that I had better figure that out too. And, of course, my casual jean days were over.

I sheepishly left his office, recognizing that we couldn't continue the meeting given his feelings.

It took me a while to process this. At first, it made me angry. Then it humbled me. Then I thought it unfair. My attire and lack of a golf game had nothing to do with my ability to serve his business needs.

Then I came to my senses. He had evaluated me based on our relationship and how I paid attention to the things that mattered to him. I needed to remodel how I operated.

This stark reality slapped me in the face and revealed a very big lesson. I thought I had ticked all the boxes—and then some—in my experience and ability to do a first-class job in servicing this client and fulfilling his requirements for our company.

Yes, the business side mattered, a lot. But first, he wanted to like me. I'm sure he saw me as much younger, but he never gave me the impression that my experience didn't measure up. He showed respect for that. He simply wanted me to show him respect in ways that were important to him. I also didn't show him the respect of doing enough homework. I should have at least assumed he enjoyed golf given that his organization had sponsored the largest PGA Tour event in the country! Ugh.

Clearly, I lacked awareness of how he would measure me.

This situation created a whole new relationship level that I had never experienced. In Europe, clients wanted to work hard and go home. Sure, social opportunities existed, but they were at highly-organized sales meetings or other planned events.

Here he asked me to take initiative to get personally involved and engage. I needed to adapt to this new evaluation system.

How did he expect to be treated?

I had to figure it out. At least he didn't show any lack of fear in letting me know where I stood.

Well, I got an earful that day, and I never made the same mistake. My wife and I found some time to go to dinner and greatly enjoyed our time with Mark and his wife. I reengaged myself with golf. And, importantly, I kept a suit in my office so that if I ever expected to see him, I had appropriate attire.

I never forgot that lesson. I recognized that in addition to doing your homework, you never know how you are being judged and when. So, do your research. Understand what is expected of you. If you are working with a new client or colleague, find out what is important to them by talking to them and those around them. You want to create success for them and yourself, so set goals in your interaction with them. Talk to them about what you want to achieve. Agree to discuss your progress. Whether this is a formal or informal process, it increases communication and understanding about what's important.

Always be clear on how you are being measured and what your criteria for success are.

It doesn't matter if your goals are personal, professional, familial, or financial. Setting goals and measuring your performance will empower you to achieve. This way, you always know where you stand in creating the success you want.

QUICK COACHING SESSION:

1. Have you ever been caught in a situation where you didn't understand how you were being measured? What did you learn?

2. How can you do some homework on a current situation you are dealing with to better understand what others expect from you?

3. Do you currently have a measurement system set up for your goals? How can you simply get one started?

CHAPTER 13

Getting Unstuck

The way to get started is to quit talking and begin doing.
—WALT DISNEY

Can you imagine a top professional golfer crying the night before playing a PGA Tournament finale that could win them $2 million?

In his book, *Golf Is Not a Game of Perfect*, sports psychologist Bob Rotella describes his professional experience helping distraught professional golfers the night before the final round of a championship. They have already played fifty-four holes and finished at the top of the leaderboard. They are already world-class players. All of them have been at the top of their game for *years*. Even then—sitting alone in their hotel room the night before the final round of the championship, overthinking things, building the stress—they let fear seep into their minds, and each becomes a bag of nerves.

They trust nothing. These are professional golfers at the top of their game, and the fear in their mind has frozen them. They cry. They want to quit. They have no confidence. And they are positive they won't be able to play golf the next morning. They are stuck and need to get unstuck.

How can they conquer this?

Does anyone doubt they can play golf? No.

Does anyone doubt they are top contenders in the world? No.

But their mind is telling them something else. Their mind is telling them they are finished. They are simply stuck. So how do they get unstuck?

One of the ways to get unstuck is to go back. Go back in time, go back into their personal history, and rebuild the sequence of stories and successes that made them who they are.

To help, Rotella takes them back to the first time they held a golf club—to the first time they smelled the grass of a freshly cut golf course. Who did they play their first round with? What did they feel when the ball went in the cup the first time? How did they progress and begin to love the game? When did they first mess around on the course with their friends, or have fun at the driving range? Where did this love of the game come from?

As you feel this original emotion seep back into your mind and your body, these core feelings push the fear aside. The love of the game takes over and overwhelms the stress associated with playing.

It's no longer about the tournament. It's no longer about all the people crowding the tee box. It's about how much they love this game and how they live to play it. They rebuild confidence by walking through the early days of learning and playing: the smells, the feelings, the successes, the teenage horseplay, the trips with their parents, the victories, the fun they had playing the game even while losing, the friends and the friendships they have built over the years.

They then recount the feelings of the successes they have already accrued as professionals. All this rebuilds their confidence and love of the game.

This coaching got these professional athletes unstuck, out of their hotel room, and back onto the golf course the next day.

You and I can follow the same process to get unstuck. Regardless of what is slowing you down, find a quiet place. Meditate for ten minutes. Take a pencil and a piece of paper and go back in your life to the early days of your development and successes. Remember the stories that created you. Remember the stories that made you feel good. What made you feel alive? What got you excited about doing what you enjoy today? Think about the successes and think about the mistakes. Laugh about them. That's right; laugh about your mistakes. Physically smile. Those mistakes have created who you are today.

Do this every day, or multiple times per day, to get yourself unstuck. This process is very simple, and it works.

I've missed more than nine thousand shots in my career. I've lost almost three hundred games. Twenty-six times, I've been trusted to take the game-winning shot and missed. I've failed over and over again, and that is why I succeed.

—MICHAEL JORDAN

Keep building on your stories and your confidence. Think about what made you who you are today—your friends, your family, your success. Fill your mind with the positive emotions of self-belief and belief in what you are doing. Consciously think forward while you fill your mind with positive feelings from the past.

Based upon what you have accomplished in your life to this date, what are some small steps you could take to move forward? What are some simple things you could do to make you 1 percent better today than you were yesterday?

One percent movement gets you unstuck. A small movement is magical. Plan out that small movement. Think about the elements of performing it. See it in your head. What is this called? It's called willing yourself forward with positive emotion.

Take a moment and blow it up big. Think of a magical moment in your life where you felt confidence. Think of a moment where you made a mistake or failed. Where were you in your life at that point? Why did it matter? What is it about the moment that struck you then and strikes you now as a part of your confidence building story? A great website to learn about storytelling and how to use it to fortify yourself is TheMoth.org.

Mine your life for meaning. Understand your story. Think through how it makes you who you are. Understand what helped build you. Write it down. Copy it again. Immerse yourself in the feelings you had when you first experienced the elements of who you are. Go back to when you were a child and you were practicing, learning how to do the things that are now part of your signature. Consider what has made you who you are today.

Don't let your mind get caught up in your failures or things that slowed you down or currently don't serve you. Spend your time thinking about the little successes and learning you experienced while you were building your knowledge, capabilities, strength, and confidence around what got you where are you are today.

Once you have planned your next small victory, go out and execute it. Make the phone call. Have the meeting. Speak with your spouse. Talk to your kids. Write the report. Have a difficult conversation. All while feeling the love and confidence of what brought you to this moment in the first place. Speak to a counselor. Get some help. All of this gets you unstuck.

QUICK COACHING SESSION:

1. Have you ever been stuck? What did you do to get out of it?

   _____
   _____
   _____
   _____
   _____
   _____

2. When you are stuck, taking just a little bit of action is movement in the right direction. Think about small actions you can take when you feel you are stagnant or have been procrastinating. What are they?

   _____
   _____
   _____
   _____
   _____
   _____

3. Stories are a powerful way to build your own confidence. What is a story about the first time you felt you were confident and were proud of an accomplishment? Implant it in your mind, and use it when you get stuck.

   _____
   _____
   _____
   _____
   _____
   _____
   _____

PART THREE

RUN TO THE FIRE

Unless you are a firefighter, no one runs to a fire.

When someone yells "fire!" in a crowded theater, everybody's trying to get out, not get in, much less run *toward* the flames. When you see a big fire, everybody is running away to avoid getting burned or even dying. In a business sense when there is a fire, you might get scorched by failure.

Big issues need big solutions. Big fires need big people. A fire is hot and difficult, and your two-million-year-old brain is screaming at you: *What if I fail? What if something goes wrong? The number of unknowns is too high, and I don't want to screw up!*

The people who run to the fire are firefighters. They are the ones who are trying to figure out how to put the fire out and save those in it. In a company, they save a business, fix the problem, breathe new life into something that isn't working, or start something fresh that is in dire need of surviving.

Let's explore that.

CHAPTER 14

What Does It Mean to Run to the Fire?

Running to the fire is about finding the courage to tackle problems head-on and to work through the discomfort that comes with growth.

—SIMON SINEK

Sure, fires are scary. But when facing them, ask yourself these questions: What if I succeed? What if I run to the fire, and I put it out or fix the problem? What's the advantage?

Overcome your fearful primitive brain as it screams, *No! Run!* It's telling you not to engage. Push that fear aside, and you will learn skills to break out of the norm as an individual and a leader. There will be new learning, opportunities, maybe a promotion, or more money. You will gain a new signature as a smart, leadership-oriented, quick-thinking team builder and capable leader.

Who wouldn't want to be known for this? I want to push you there. I want you to find fires that make sense to run to.

Nothing ventured, nothing gained.

Coming out of business school at Notre Dame, I had an exciting job offer from a global advertising agency. During the arduous interview process, I really fell in love with the company, its people, and the advertising industry. In this role, I would get major league marketing and advertising experience on big recognizable brands. The prospect of building high-level relationships with large clients made the opportunity ever more exciting. I practically jumped out of my shoes when I got the offer.

Only one sticking point remained.

A controversial cigarette company stood at the top of the list as their largest client.

For some, this might not matter. I have had many colleagues who worked in advertising and marketing for a host of industries that sold products legally but that one might have an ethical aversion for: liquor, cigarettes, contraception, etc. Absolutely nothing is wrong with any of it.

But I had no interest in selling cigarettes.

The big cigarette client, with the obvious smoking-related moral issue, slowed me down in accepting the job. I even spoke to my ethics professor, a Catholic priest, for guidance.

In the end, external guidance helped me simplify the dilemma: As long as I didn't participate in creating the marketing and advertising for the cigarette brands, I could work for the agency. Although still slightly uneasy, I found the ethical situation of the organization having a cigarette client acceptable. I made the decision to take the job based on the assurance that if I didn't want to work on cigarette advertising, I wouldn't have to. Good enough for me.

Fast forward ten years.

I had started my career in the US, then moved to Frankfurt, and on to Copenhagen in a variety of roles with growing authority. I excelled and absolutely loved the lifestyle, languages, and cultures. My family and career thrived.

Late one Tuesday night, I got a phone call from the European CEO. He asked me to take on the top job as the Sweden-based managing director, my first office leadership role. Senior management difficulties plagued the office at that time, and those gentlemen were leaving the agency—the next day. The CEO wanted me there.

A quick turnaround.

Soon after my arrival—and in the whirlwind of trying to figure out the issues, gauge the morale of my new team, and understand client needs—my financial director pulled me aside and told me that she had prepared payroll for the following week, and we weren't going to have enough money to pay everyone.

Hmm, an interesting dilemma, I thought. There I stood, parachuted into a fire, in a global firm I had worked with for ten years in four countries, and we had no money. Why couldn't we make payroll?

Well, it seemed we'd paid off the executives that were let go, but someone forgot to do the math along the way. The severance payoffs made the previous day had drained the bank account.

At that time, wiring money around the world from the corporate head office didn't happen instantaneously on your phone. Approvals were necessary. Explanations took time. We couldn't get it done—at least not in time to make payroll. Our local bank wouldn't give us the money because we had just fired the local management and put an American in their place to fix the business problem. We found ourselves in quite a predicament.

Turning this office around meant I needed to build trust with the team, and not much trust gets built when you tell your people you can't afford to pay them. I simply had no choice but to find a creative solution. The finance director and I shuffled through several potential quick fixes but couldn't find anything that would produce the cash we needed in the timeframe required.

So, keeping the payroll problem quiet, I took the initiative to call a "new business opportunities" meeting. Pulling the team together as I sat nervously in the IKEA chair we'd just put together the day before, I asked the team if any of our global firm's international clients would possibly be interested in working with us in Sweden.

A colleague and friend of mine, Klaus, a senior executive in the office, looked at me thoughtfully as he took a drag on his hand-rolled Drum cigarette. He sat up and boldly blew a puff of smoke in my face with a mischievous smile.

Then he answered: "Cigarettes."

Klaus understood how I felt about working for a cigarette client. He would visit Sue and me at our place when we worked together back in Frankfurt. I would stand outside and chat with him as he had a cigarette on our terrace. He knew my "I won't work at this company if I have to sell cigarettes" story. Although Klaus loved to smoke, I found he had the same ethical aversion to selling them.

So, he sat there shocked in Sweden when I said, "Call them up, and let's set up a meeting!"

This client, delighted that we had called, invited us over immediately. They hadn't heard from the agency in the couple years since we opened our doors in that market (it seems prior management didn't want to work with them either). They had three new projects they desperately needed help with. We worked all night to prepare the briefs, and brazenly asked for up-front payment of 50 percent of the fee to start the three projects. Without batting an eye, they handed us a check, and we deposited it at our friendly local bank—just in time for payday.

I suppose it would be easy to judge me in this situation. My ethics crumbled when the going got tough. I should have found another way. I didn't stand up for what I believed in.

Call me shallow, but none of that bothered me much.

What mattered most? My people. What's the big leadership lesson? It's not about me. Serving my team to make sure they got paid mattered more to me than grinding my teeth over whether I wanted to work with a cigarette client. I ran to the fire and solved the problem. As you can see, running to the fire means you will be stretched in ways you never thought possible. I learned a lot in fighting that fire.

Running to the fire can be physically, mentally, and ethically challenging. That's why it provides the greatest path to learning, problem solving, and effectively dealing with adversity. Running to the fire puts you to the test: It stresses your leadership, it makes you find people to help, and it inspires others to achieve and share the victory.

QUICK COACHING SESSION:

1. Have you recognized opportunities to run to the fire? Did you say yes?

2. What new skills did you learn?

3. Do you see the professional value of running to the fire while others are running away?

CHAPTER 15

Which Fires Do I Run To?

We shall go on to the end, we shall fight in France, we shall fight on the seas and oceans, we shall fight with growing confidence and growing strength in the air, we shall defend our Island, whatever the cost may be, we shall fight on the beaches, we shall fight on the landing grounds, we shall fight in the fields and in the streets, we shall fight in the hills; we shall never surrender.

—WINSTON CHURCHILL

Once US Secretary of State, Colin Powell gives this advice for running to a fire: "Use the formula P=40 to 70, in which P stands for the probability of success and the numbers indicate the percentage of information acquired. Once the information is in the 40 to 70 percent range, go with your gut."

So acquire at least 40 percent of the information, and don't waste time grubbing for 100 percent of it. It takes too long. Get smart, fast.

In offering you this insight, I am not telling you to run to every fire, leap in, and start firefighting. You always need to analyze first, and then act. The more knowledgeable you are, the more capable you are, the more learning you have prepared yourself with, and the more corners you have looked around, the more ready you are to take on a fire fight.

By running to the fire, you'll get personal growth—win or lose. You'll live to fight another day, you'll discover others with the same disposition, you'll go into battles with teammates, and you'll build lasting bonds that will serve you throughout your career. You will also develop leadership skills that will enhance your growth, income, resilience, capability, and respect.

Problem solving + adversity = faster growth and success.

Sure, running to the fire means taking a risk. But managing your career and its growth trajectory is about managing risk. You manage risk by getting smart. You manage risk by doing your homework. You manage risk by taking on more projects that allow you to learn more than the other person does. You manage risk by learning and reading and hearing about others who took risks.

My instance of firefighting in Sweden led to taking over bigger problem clients and turning them around, as well as taking over startup companies and multiplying their size. As an entrepreneur I gained the skills, confidence, and foresight to turn around a global company and rebuild it. Being able to do so built the confidence and capability to start my own company, acquire six organizations, and build the business to 350 people from scratch.

Running to the fire is powerful. It creates the person you were meant to be.

Did I make mistakes? Yes! Did I fail at some tasks? Yes! Did I wonder what the heck I got myself into? Yes! Did it cause stress for me and my family? Yes!

But I paid attention to the importance of the moment, and I learned from it.

Running to the fire is like being in the championship game. Some folks shrink from it, and some fill the space and create victory. In the latter, you will develop superior problem solving and resiliency skills that will rival the levels achieved by pro athletes. Your colleagues will marvel at your growth as you pass them by.

Most people do not run to the fire. The overwhelming majority shy away and let others step in and fix stuff before they tiptoe into some smoldering embers to help. Look for fires you know you can put out, and leverage them into opportunities for growth.

QUICK COACHING SESSION:

1. Do you have opportunities to run to the fire right now? What are the risks?

   _____
   _____
   _____
   _____
   _____
   _____
   _____

2. What do you think you could learn if you got up right now to seek the heat?

   _____
   _____
   _____
   _____
   _____
   _____
   _____

3. Have you turned down opportunities to run to the fire? Why?

   _____
   _____
   _____
   _____
   _____
   _____
   _____

CHAPTER 16

Choose Your Team Carefully

To build a great team, you must first attract the right people. And just as importantly, you must keep the wrong people from joining your team.

—JIM COLLINS

Probably the most important part of leadership and success is choosing and leading a team. In my experience, making the right team choice centers on three key elements.

First, prioritize diversity. Do not choose people who look, think, and act like you. Think about the task at hand and about the kinds of skill sets necessary to solve it in an above-and-beyond manner. Seek out the people who can make that happen. Recognize that you will have leadership growth in bringing that team together and helping it to work. Different personalities, capabilities, and dispositions are magic in problem solving—if they can be managed correctly.

Second, ensure psychological safety for your group. This highly effective team of thoroughbreds kicking in the stalls needs to have an outlet. They need to be able to say what they feel. They need confidentiality. They need psychological safety that allows them to share, vent, and talk about problems and issues openly. That's how you get to solutions faster. If people are afraid to speak, they won't.

Third, your team members need to be able to inspire each other. Whether it's their positive attitude, the quality of their work, or their ability to build rapport quickly, they need to work well together and fit as a team. An inspired group works toward achieving ten times what they think they can. An uninspired group never gets off the ground. It is incredible to think about the difference.

How do you find this team? Who should you look for?

Look around corners as you think of potential opportunities for growth. If you said yes to an opportunity and now need to build a team, here are some questions to ask yourself:

- Who would you love to work with?
- Who do you work well with that has a complementary skill set?
- Who is quiet but wicked smart?
- Who can keep the group on task?
- Who has great field knowledge?
- Who has sales ability?
- Who has presentation skills?
- Who has analytical or programming capability?

- Who is a leader?
- Who is the smartest, most amazing pain in the ass you think could benefit the group?

Let's assume you have followed my advice above and chosen a crack team. Here are eight key actions to build teamwork quickly and keep them performing at a high level:

1. Never leave anyone hanging out to dry. Monitor how everyone works together and foster growth.
2. Communicate, communicate, communicate.
3. Let them think and solve problems. Give them the freedom. They will have ideas and capabilities far beyond your own.
4. Bring them pizza, and serve them Krispy Kreme donuts when necessary.
5. Create small victories to celebrate, so the team goes from victory to victory. And when a setback arises, celebrate the setback because it has led to learning.
6. Reiterate that learning comes from both wins *and* losses. The best learning comes from the challenges.
7. If someone doesn't fit, act quickly. You don't have time to lose. Iterate and find the right team, and always talk about what you are learning.
8. Openly teach insight learned from challenging situations. Don't only discuss things amongst those who were involved; make sure the whole team knows. Of the many mistakes I've made in my career, the biggest ones were to not analyze wins and losses enough to consciously seek insight. I often mistook speed for success and shrugged off losses and mistakes without analyzing them to find the nuggets.

Build your team with excellence in mind. You never know when you might need them.

Often, though, you won't get to have a say in choosing your team. What then?

In attacking this situation, analyze it. What are the tasks? What are the needs? Line them up with the people you have available for fighting this fire. Be open. Talk about the issues. What is your team's current ability to move forward? What are you missing? Do you have an opportunity to augment your team? Does the team currently have members who don't work well together or don't have the necessary skill sets?

Openly conveying what is happening when you are in this situation is very important. Lay out your program as you figure it out, and communicate it. Make the team a part of the process. Inspire the group, lead them, monitor them, and develop trust while establishing clear priorities. Constantly evaluate and reevaluate whether you have the right folks on the bus.

Although you may not have had the initial choice of this team, the opportunity to excel and to upgrade always arises.

QUICK COACHING SESSION:

1. Make a list of five top-caliber people who would be your first choices when building any team.

   _____
   _____
   _____
   _____
   _____
   _____

2. What would this group be good at?

   _____
   _____
   _____
   _____
   _____
   _____

3. Have you ever seen the value of a quiet team member? Or someone who is a little tougher to get along with? How can being understanding of differences help you assemble a great team?

   _____
   _____
   _____
   _____
   _____
   _____
   _____

CHAPTER 17

Say Yes and Figure It Out

If somebody offers you an amazing opportunity but you are not sure you can do it, say yes—then learn how to do it later!
—RICHARD BRANSON

Richard Branson started Virgin Records in 1972 while running a fledgling mail-order record business called Virgin. He sold records by mail and struggled with how to grow. He met a musician, Mike Oldfield, whose album *Tubular Bells* had been rejected by every record label Oldfield had spoken to. But Branson loved the album and thought it could be a potential hit.

When no other record executives saw the album's potential, he saw an opportunity to start his own record label to produce it. Branson decided to release it himself under the newly formed Virgin Records label. *Tubular Bells* went on to become a massive success and helped launch Virgin Records as a major player in the music industry.

Branson had no idea how to create, launch, or run a record label. One could argue that he also had little idea how to judge if a particular album would have any commercial value. He saw a means to an end with *Tubular Bells*. He liked the music and saw a path to more importance in the industry than simply selling albums in the mail. He said yes first and figured it out as he went.

Have you ever been stuck saying yes to something, and you had no idea how you would get it done? Whether you say yes out of guilt or not wanting to look bad or to show that you earnestly wanted to be in the game, it's done.

I had just taken over the troubled startup Canadian office of a global agency. On the positive side, it had some good people and one very good client. Unfortunately, that didn't constitute success. I needed to clean things up and build the business to turn things around quickly. I felt the biggest opportunity lay with that one good client. Like we've learned: build on existing strengths.

Following my mediocre play on the golf course with one of the executives of a large Canadian automotive client (yes, by this time I had taken some golf lessons and came to accept "business golf"), I checked my voicemail. I had received a call from the US division leader of that automotive client, who I had met only briefly at an event. He asked if I might call him back.

Ecstatic with the perceived potential of the call, I struggled to get my golf glove off to dial the number. When we connected, he offered us an astonishing opportunity—to pitch their direct marketing business.

More specifically, he said, "You are doing such a great job in Canada that we wanted to see if you were interested in pitching our business in the US. There could be some good synergies for us internally."

I couldn't believe my luck. On the other end of the phone was the possibility of being a major marketing partner of a top ten global auto company. Amazing! As I considered it for another ten seconds while he spoke, it began to scare me to death. We were a company of twenty-five people. Winning that account would immediately increase the size of our agency fivefold.

He probed further, "I know your agency is smaller, like most Canadian companies compared to US firms. Do you have the capability to handle our needs?"

Their needs, to execute development of direct mail campaigns in the tens of millions, were massive. At this point, we had only handled campaigns in the tens of thousands.

I answered truthfully, but somewhat cagily, "We are very capable, with a creative, knowledgeable staff in every area you require. Yes, we can handle it, and I can prove it. It's the core of what we do."

Although their demand fell in our sweet spot, we had no idea how to handle this extreme level of scale.

But I said yes.

My team did end up proving what I'd claimed. We pitched for and won that business against four other competitors ten times our size. It transformed us and launched a new level of success for our organization. It quintupled the size of the business overnight. We could hire people who knew how to execute a program of that size, understood the data requirements, and had the expertise necessary to craft a program that would substantially grow the client's business.

By the time we won that account and added several other initiatives from that client, the growth ended up contributing to a tenfold increase in our revenue. It also created global opportunities for us and helped us grow in stature at home, so we won more local business with a greatly enhanced profile.

None of it would have gotten off the ground without saying a trembling, slightly fearful, "Yes."

Here and now, talking about how I said yes and figured it out is easy, but what does that really mean?

It means the real work starts: the meticulous planning, the building of the right and ready team, the leadership with vision and inspiration for the team and the client. Now is the time for showing strength in every area of knowledge and capability, building relationships and partnerships with smart people, and understanding the needs of the client and the needs of your team.

Lastly and probably most importantly, now is the time to lead with belief. You must believe you can get this done. You must believe your team can come together and create awe-inspiring work that will change perspectives. When you believe, others will follow. And partnerships will spring up where you never expected them.

As we were grinding away in the process of winning this pitch, we progressed through several hurdles. We persevered for six months through countless presentations, pricing bids, repricing bids, and best and final bids. We hung on until the client neared an announcement of who would win the business. A victory would be amazing, but it would also require an immense amount of investment in hardware, software, and people. The client wanted to scale up quickly, as they always do, and this would be very challenging for us.

One day, while pacing in my office and trying to figure all of this out, our highly capable IT partner and CEO, Steve Simmons, ambled into my office. Easy-going Steve never looked worried.

"I have been working with your team, and I understand what your issues are in terms of scaling the hardware, software, and programming for this big CRM program," Steve said. "I know it's a monster, and I think I might have a solution for you."

My ears doubled in size. We had already pushed a lot of water uphill to get this far in this onerous process. Hearing a partner think alongside me was music to my ears. I needed all the help I could get. Steve came up with an entrepreneurial

IT strategy where he would go out and fund the hardware and software build entirely on his own, partnering with our organization to put this together.

Rather than my company having to come up with all the cash to purchase the equipment and software, Steve purchased it and simply allowed me to lease from him. This sort of arrangement might be normal today, but at that time it shifted the earth for me. He conceived a well-thought-through and visionary program that transformed our ability to execute very quickly on a large scale.

Even more unbelievably, Steve recognized this had to be executed almost immediately following the announcement of the winner. He'd had such confidence we were going to win that he started planning forward without any guarantee of business.

All he needed was a handshake.

Luckily, Steve's entrepreneurial spirit gave him license to believe in what we were doing. So much so that he approached friends and family to raise money so that he could purchase the hardware to deliver the program for us. Steve stepped up because he believed. He saw how we said yes then figured it out, so he followed suit.

When you believe, others believe. And when others believe, great things happen.

When I said yes, did I worry if I would fail? Humbly stated, not really. At this point in my career, I already had enough success and learning to build confidence that I could figure it out. But I didn't want to let the team down. This is what really drove me.

Looking back, so many things could have derailed our bid for the account. But in the moment, I didn't let our size, or the impossible notion that a tiny Canadian agency could win a massive marketing program for a big car company, slow me down.

Everyone on that team learned that saying yes and figuring it out is an awesome experience. I wanted them to have that. And it launched a whole new generation of people in the organization to a new level.

Saying yes can create big and heretofore unknown opportunities for you and your people. It will challenge you, push your knowledge, scare you, and escalate your learning. You will discover that you and those around you are much more capable than you thought.

Ready to start his luxury home construction business, North Fork Builders of Montana, Jon Evans pounded the pavement looking for projects to get the new company off the ground. He had a meeting set up with a prominent architect who did brilliant design work on luxury homes across the country. Jon had enjoyed a good relationship with him through his past employer and tried desperately to get his first project from him. The country, suffering from a deep recession, did not offer much opportunity for luxury home builders at the time. That didn't deter Jon.

The architect regarded Jon highly for his work and wanted to help him get his new gig off the ground. That said, he always counseled his clients to choose a first-class builder, not typically a startup.

As Jon made his pitch, the architect listened and finally smiled. He trusted Jon. He knew he could do great work, and he believed in him.

With a great sigh, the architect laid out his dilemma, "Jon, I've got a project for you. But it's not in Montana. It's 1,300 miles away—in Wisconsin. Can you put together a remote crew to build an immense legacy home, that will take four years to complete, for one of America's most successful industrial families?

Wow. This project, a dream for any construction company, had landed in the lap of a guy whose company hadn't built even one house yet. It would have been easy to beg off and politely say no—too big, too far away, too hard to manage, too much for a startup. Imagine the difficulty trying to manage something like that from 1,300 miles away.

Well, Jon wouldn't be in this book had he said no. Jon said yes and figured it out. Saying yes launched his successful construction business from scratch fifteen years ago, and today he employs 125 people and is a premier luxury home builder in Montana. Jon stepped up and never looked back. It took perseverance and grit to get that done. He built the team who could build a dream house for that family.

Good things happen when you have the courage to say yes.

QUICK COACHING SESSION:

1. Do you have any regrets from saying no to an opportunity?

2. Make a list and identify the opportunity cost of saying no.

3. Can you say yes to anything right now?

4. Make a list of the times you said yes, and catalogue the confidence and learning you gained from it.

CHAPTER 18

Confront Stuff, Look Around Corners, and Believe

I'd put my money on the sun and solar energy. What a source of power! I hope we don't have to wait until oil and coal run out before we tackle that. I wish I had more years left.
—THOMAS EDISON

Talk about seeing around corners.

Seeing around corners is thinking through "what ifs." What if we win that big account? What if we lose an account and have financial difficulty? What if the software doesn't work? What if our system shuts down and we can't process customer data?

Analyze possible problems. Go down the decision tree on what might happen if certain things were to become a possibility. Thinking through scenarios like this allows you to get in front of potential issues so that you can solve them quickly—because you are thinking about them, and others aren't.

Put the fires out when they are small.

This is not about focusing on being right. Instead, this centers on creating opportunities and expanding your perspective—so as new information becomes available, you are prepared to act.

Take a good look at your business and what influences it internally and externally. Look at economic indicators. Look at a client issue that has gone unresolved. Recognize poor customer service and what it could lead to. Notice surprising data that could indicate a problem. Could a poor relationship in the organization backfire? Could negative social media about an individual or the company create a problem?

Think about doomsday scenarios as well as great upside opportunities. Use that information to build some realistic scenarios that include both an upside and a downside. This will create a new understanding of the influences on the business. It will also help you to see around corners and find out what could be coming at you. Do "what if" sessions with your team. Have conversations about the potential issues. This builds perspective in everyone. As you engage in this thought process, you will notice important things begin to happen. Your team builds trust, and you trust yourself more too.

Now put it to use. You are smarter. You can notice things because you put the effort in. You have looked at the variables, so spotting a problem is easier, whether big or small. When you notice small problems, you can act. To put out fires, you need to confront them.

Try to take action when issues and problems are still small. Seek them out and solve them. Develop that capability, mindset, and skill set in your team.

The magic potion that got NASA to the moon involved an endless number of engineers working through "what ifs." They spent every waking hour thinking of everything that could go wrong before Apollo launched. Once they figured out the thousands of things that could go wrong, they developed solutions and sequencing for them—literally thousands of procedures. That's how they figured out what to do right. While you're practicing and failing, you see opportunity and can confront it by developing solutions (Hadfield 2014).

You will understand when something is out of whack and can imagine solutions. You will believe you are smart enough and driven enough to fix it—and so will your team. You will believe that you are the right person to tackle it. People will clearly see that confronting and solving the problem is very important to the future of your team and the future of the organization.

Now, you may be the only person seeing the future and trying to do something about it preemptively. Don't worry about being labeled a crazy person who chases every little ghost. When you spend the time making the effort to expand your understanding, learning, and experience, you will see only the legitimate issues and problems—and you will see them faster than others. You will be able to act with surety.

Believe me—plenty of issues in business today go unnoticed and unsolved when they are small, and these issues create big inferno problems later. Unfortunately, it's often human nature to avoid small issues until they become big and less easily solved—or at least a lot more time-consuming and expensive.

Trust yourself and believe.

QUICK COACHING SESSION:

1. What information do you have available for you to spend some time strategically looking around corners? What do you see?

2. Can you identify anything today that requires your attention?

3. Put together a group of "what if" questions on a current project you have. Does asking the questions help you to see something you hadn't seen before?

CHAPTER 19

You Must Be Nuts

"You'll never accomplish that."
"I don't know what you're thinking."
"I can't believe you think you could be successful."
"Do you understand the risk? This could ruin your career!"

If you think you can accomplish something great, you must be nuts.

Confidence is a necessary, powerful, difference-making tool in your personal power arsenal. Without it you won't accomplish much. Getting out of your comfort zone, taking on new challenges, or living your life beyond simple nonthreatening decision making will be tough.

In the interest of improving yourself, having confidence to probe who you are and what you are capable of is a very good thing. Confidence leads to taking some risk, accomplishing difficult tasks, and learning from that success. It builds each time you do it.

If you think of a child learning to walk, you see this confidence-building phenomenon. They learn a little bit each day. They gain confidence as they see and feel what they can accomplish. They take little risks. They fall. They cry. They get back up again. The process continues until walking becomes second nature. Then they are confident they can do it. And they search for the next challenge.

Searching for success is important in all aspects of your life—personal, family, and business. And it really is your duty to put forth the effort to learn what you can and push for your best version of success. Doing this is critical for your sense of self and your ability to believe you can help others.

Some confidence-building moments take on a new dimension. I call them "you must be nuts" moments. Sometimes when you set off to do something, others will think you're crazy. You will hear things like:

"You must be nuts for thinking you can do that!"

These are difficult, often belittling moments, delivered by friends, colleagues, and family, that we must have the confidence to push through.

I accepted a transfer to Germany early in my career at least in part because I had spent a year in undergrad in Germany and Austria working hard to learn the language and really enjoyed exploring the culture and traveling in Europe. As Sue had spent a portion of her undergraduate studies in Copenhagen and had lived in Sweden as an exchange student, she was equally excited about the opportunity to live in Europe.

A large multinational client wanted to hire our agency in Germany. That office needed someone with relevant experience and language skills to start the relationship and lead the account. Word quickly got out at the corporate office that my next promotion involved a transfer to Frankfurt.

This created my first "you must be nuts" moment in business.

The naysayers came out of the woodwork. Now, I don't want you to think that everyone spouted negative comments. Most people were positive and offered their best wishes. But in many moments some smart, more experienced colleagues questioned my judgment. Each of the following questions were prefaced with "you must be nuts!"

"I could never do that. How will you speak the language to clients? Won't you sound like a first grader in a presentation?"

"What happens if things don't work out for you over there? Do you think they will allow you to transfer back here?"

"What happens if you get there and you don't like it? Can you come back?"

"Is there an opportunity for you to stay with the company if your boss doesn't like you?"

This surprised me. But if I look at it thoughtfully now, I suppose all of this "you must be nuts" negativism served a purpose in that I hadn't really contemplated many of these questions before. Some of them were very good. Although I read most of them as others foisting their fear on me, they did help me to think more critically about the move and what some of the risks were.

I believed I could figure things out. I had excellent training and understood the client's business in the US. What I needed to learn was the local client and consumer. Even so, I had lived in Germany as a student, understood the culture, and had confidence in my ability to do the job. The most excitement lay in getting along with my new colleagues, being able to learn the language more deeply, and Sue and I enjoying our life there.

After having discussed some of these questions with Sue, we decided to go for it. We were going to make the best of it. I didn't allow the negativism in others to paralyze me. It could very clearly have stopped me in my tracks. These were big, important issues I had seen happen to people. Even in my short time in business, I knew they were real.

I decided I could not allow external fears to kill the opportunity. Their fear created "you must be nuts," not mine. Those who were trying to "help" me were fearfully forcing their own lack of self-confidence on me. I wanted to go down the rabbit hole, and I can imagine a few of them were jealous I had this opportunity and wanted to slow me down. Such is life in the corporate world.

So, in good form and ready for anything, we packed up our house, got on the plane to Germany, and walked right into what became the biggest career opportunity of my life.

Remember, those who say "you must be nuts" are often the same people who will later say "I wish I had done that" when they see your success.

QUICK COACHING SESSION:

1. Have you ever been criticized for taking decisive action? Did it fuel you or drag you down?

2. Think of a time when you were berated for taking advantage of an opportunity. Think past what others said, and find your own personal power in that moment. Did you move forward with the action? Did you find success?

3. Does someone in your life act critical too often when you take action that scares them? Should you let them go and find others who can support you?

PART FOUR

MANAGE UP

Managing up is the key to success. If you can't manage the people above you, you'll have difficulty managing the people below you to success.

—DANA ROUSMANIERE

Managing up might seem like groveling at your boss's feet. It's not. Managing up, simply put, is smartly staying connected to your boss or those who have influence over you. That could be a classic boss, a client, or a customer. That could also be a board or some other group of people who is involved in evaluating what you're doing or is integral to your success and your organization's success.

Everybody has a boss.

Often, high performers are not great communicators. Although I believed I had great communication skills, not communicating became a problem for me. I moved quickly, used my instincts, and got great results. I thought my results would speak for themselves. Being highly motivated, I decided I would rather keep pushing for results than waste time writing reports to my boss to bring them up to speed on all my success.

For some of my bosses, that worked. I tended to spend more time with the ones I liked. They knew what I achieved and appreciated how it made them look good. The ones I didn't like so much, well…

This practice generated the big problem.

Given that everyone has a boss, and I have had many in my career, when I came across one that didn't see things like I did or seemed threatened by me or didn't like me, I simply steered clear of them. I didn't stop to realize that my boss had their own expectations. They had their own dreams. They spent their own time trying to figure out how to get ahead.

As one of their direct reports, I should have found it always proper and necessary to spend time bringing them up to speed or, as I have called this part of the book, managing up.

Managing up is not a choice. It's a necessity. Let's talk about what that means.

CHAPTER 20

Don't Let Your Ego Get the Best of You

The ego is the single biggest obstruction to the achievement of anything.

—RICHARD ROSE

My ego often got the best of me. But it only truly threatened my job once.

I had great success working in the agency's international division for almost ten years. Having risen quickly in the ranks, I helped grow sizable accounts and performed a few turnarounds with both offices and clients. I rocked and felt very confident in my ability to create success. Unfortunately, I let my ego swell a bit, and it got me in trouble.

An opportunity arose to move back to the US for a big promotion to senior vice president. This key role in the corporate headquarters positioned me to run the largest account in the US agency. The account had suffered some difficulty (my specialty), and senior agency management recruited me to transfer back to the US to fix it.

Leading a big US account meant I would report to the global head. But this leader had a controversial past and did not handle people well. He had a big ego and a poor reputation. That's where I made my first mistake. In my mind, as global head of the business, the problems had developed under his watch. And he hadn't solved them.

He played nice with me to get me to take the job. I chose to believe him and internally discounted, or at least downplayed, the information I had about his lousy management style. I knew my capabilities and felt I could get around him. I had made a career of dealing with difficult people. This is when my ego started to play a role. I figured, if things got difficult, I could just straight-arm him and bulldoze ahead. *I am that good*, I thought. Besides, senior management brought *me* in to solve *his* problem, right?

Unfortunately, that's not how things turned out. The more I pushed, the more he pushed back. He had a bombastic, egomaniacal style, and it really put me off. I am sure I made him angry too. That said, I convinced myself my actions were proper because I prided myself on caring for and supporting my people and delivering first-class work to my clients. In my mind, he didn't care about any of that. He just cared about himself. My do-the-right-thing attitude fueled me, but he didn't care.

So, I just kept believing in myself, spending less and less time with him. The already-bad relationship kept getting worse.

Finally, we had a couple shouting sessions, which of course he won. The horror of the situation began to hit me: I lived in misery. I had made this bed and couldn't get out of it.

He was the boss. Unbelievably, I seldom treated him like one.

After months of turmoil, I began to realize that I got stuck in a situation I could not win—one that my ego had led me to believe I could.

I eventually got offered another opportunity, and I took it to get away from this toxic boss.

The next span turned out to be a very interesting time in my career. I had enjoyed a fair amount of success and, as I rose in the organization, the playing field kept getting bigger and the stakes higher. Unfortunately, the personalities I had to deal with also became bigger. I didn't really spend enough time contemplating how to navigate this. I hated company politics but never realized that politics simply meant people and their point of view. These were important relationships I needed to develop. But either my ego, immaturity, or simple dislike of the people stopped me from seeing it.

I did not accept the responsibility for making sure I managed up. I only went to see my boss when he demanded it. I didn't spend any time in his office keeping him abreast of issues, nor did I spend time with him traveling or socially. Essentially, I gave him very little because I didn't like him.

When that sort of thing happens, your boss goes to other sources of information to find out how you're doing. This is not a good scenario. They draw their own conclusions, or they listen to the conclusions that others have drawn. You want to be in control of the information as well as your performance. You want to be able to tell the truth about how you're doing, how you feel, how it's impacting the company, and how it's impacting your boss.

You also need to give your boss a heads up in case you need the field cleared for something you would like to undertake. You need to inform them about your goals and aspirations, as well as your great ideas. You can't do that if your ego is driving you in the wrong direction.

If your ego is getting in the way, then you think you are better than you are. And if you *are* better than you are, and you don't tell anybody… it's a secret. Use your skills and personal power for the good of everyone around you, including your boss. If you don't, you are in the game only for yourself—and that doesn't end well.

In any leadership context, stay humble. Keep track of what and how you are doing. Make and take regular meetings with your boss to keep them abreast of what's going on. Build a relationship. Get to know them. Your initial negative judgment may be incorrect. Always leave your ego at the door.

QUICK COACHING SESSION:

1. Think about a situation where you thought you were "too good" to waste time developing a relationship with a colleague or boss. Did you find success?

2. When you feel like you are better than someone, what are some steps you can take to get out of that mindset and tone down your ego?

CHAPTER 21

Know Your Numbers

Numbers are the highest degree of knowledge. It is knowledge itself.

—PLATO

Business is built on numbers.

They are the single most effective way to keep track of what is going on. If your business is worth engaging in, key numbers play a role in monitoring it. Whether it is sales, profitability, expenses, assets, liabilities, or some variation thereupon that pertains to you, your role, or your division in the company—you need to own these numbers.

Numbers are the goalpost, the measuring stick, and the guideline to your success as well as the business's success. And guess what? Your boss cares a lot about the numbers. This person is gauged, judged, and evaluated by the numbers probably even more than you are because their stature in the company is higher than yours. If the boss doesn't hit their numbers, then everyone has a problem.

Knowing your numbers and how you contribute to the business is paramount in your relationship with your boss. If you don't know your numbers, they will think you are either neglecting them, don't know or understand them, or think there's no need to know them. You do not want any of these. Spending time with your boss, sharing the numbers, and going through challenges, wins, and losses is a great opportunity to find out where they want to go and where you need to go.

In one of my first senior leadership roles, I went into a meeting with the managing director and the finance director. I had just been promoted and had managed large clients—but had not had access to, or responsibility for, the corporate P&L (profit and loss) statement. I can recall sitting in the meeting and being quiet, looking at the numbers and trying to make sense of them. Some were projections and budget-related, and others were what we had already achieved. My brain worked overtime trying to make heads and tails of how it all worked together.

I didn't have any experience with the agency's financial management. So, what did I do? I took this book of numbers home, and I slept with it.

Literally.

I woke up in the morning studying those numbers, and I went to bed at night studying those numbers. It got to the point where I dreamt about those numbers. Thank goodness my wife understood!

I dove deeply into learning the relationship between important trends and tried to understand how they worked. If a client increased spending or indicated they were going to increase spending, I needed to understand how this progressed through the profit and loss statement. How we tracked our costs and serviced the client also had a big impact on our profitability.

I asked a lot of questions, and I did a lot of analysis. Just looking at the numbers didn't satisfy me. I struggled. I really needed to understand the meaning behind them. That takes experience studying them, asking questions in the organization to find out what's really going on, and watching the real-world action take place. That's the ideal situation: when you can put two plus two together to make sure it equals four.

Understanding those numbers also helps you see around corners. If revenue is slowing down, you need to know where to act on your expenses. If one client looks like their spending is slowing down and another is going to increase, you need to think about whether the same resources can service a different client. Those are only two simple parts to this, but understanding how the business worked and combining that with new knowledge of the financials allowed me to take the first steps to become a much better manager.

This increased my business acuity and made me a smarter leader when I walked into the boss's office.

If you own the financials, take responsibility for them, and understand what's behind them, you can properly discuss and develop perspective about what you think the future will hold. You become a superior asset in your organization.

And you are doing a great job managing up.

QUICK COACHING SESSION:

1. What are the numbers that drive your business? Do you understand them? Do you know where to get them?

　

2. As you look at the numbers, try to draw relationships between them. How do they interact? Are some number relationships more important than others?

　

3. Can you find a colleague, mentor, or leader in your organization to discuss the numbers with?

CHAPTER 22

Are You a Threat?

One of my mentors taught me, "A boss is never threatened by a subordinate who does just enough to get by. They're threatened by those who consistently exceed expectations."

It's not untypical to think if you are a high performer that you are capable, likable, open-minded, and a good leader. You may not be at all cognizant of the fact that all these smarts rolled up into a ball of energy and performance could be a threat to someone.

Not the least your boss.

Your boss should get the benefit of all that performance, shouldn't they? Why would they think you would be a threat to them? Human nature is human nature. Your boss may feel intimidated by your knowledge, skills, or abilities and see you as a potential rival or threat to their own position. They may feel threatened by your independence, autonomy, or ability to take initiative, and may see you as a challenge to their own authority or control. Your boss may feel threatened by your career aspirations and see you as a potential obstacle to their own plans or ambitions.

You need to understand and contemplate that this is a possibility if you are having difficulty building a relationship with your boss.

Does your reputation precede you? Have others spoken about you to your boss and instilled some fear as to whether you will be a team player? Sure, good bosses want producers, but lousy bosses can be threatened by this. How do you solve being too good and potentially a threat to your boss?

You need to get on board and show your boss that all your performance is for them. You need to manage up effectively. You need to understand your boss's priorities, deliver on those priorities, always be prepared, and display commitment. You need to take away the threat. If it's important for you to talk about that threat with your boss, then talk about it. The key thing to understand is that being perceived as a threat is real.

You can be a threat to anyone, but being a threat to your boss is a threat to your job.

Understand that, seek to understand your boss's priorities, and deliver on them. Spend more time than you normally would in their office showing your commitment and your understanding of their priorities. Show that you can work for them and you are both driven by the same level of success.

I realize this is a lot of work. And it might seem like I'm telling you to bend over backward for difficult people.

Remember, stay humble. Assume best intentions and assume that your boss, though possibly threatened by you, wants the same thing you want. Do what you can to build relationships and to deliver on priorities and your commitment.

If all this fails, people typically leave the job. What's unfortunate about this—and is endemic in some organizations that no longer train their leaders or foster any kind of performance metrics—is that good people leave lousy leadership.

I suggest you stick it out longer. If you are working with a great company that you love and you have good colleagues and you like the leadership, don't leave at the first sign of difficulty with your boss. Find a mentor in the organization. Hire a coach outside the organization. Use these people to help you focus and be accountable to the things that matter and take their guidance in helping you manage up to a difficult boss. Don't just walk away from the job if the boss sucks.

Although I'm sure there are plenty of stories to suggest the contrary, bad leadership usually doesn't last very long. Stick it out, and if it continues, consider a transfer or a new project or some other opportunity within the organization that you could be connected to through a mentor or your own networking.

I hope to serve you and not to tell you to hang on to a lousy boss or organization forever. If it's a great organization, stick with it. Work to deliver for your boss. Get help to work through it. Both you and your boss will learn from the experience.

Another boss I experienced harbored the qualities of a lousy, disrespectful leader. He chose favorites, didn't foster exemplary work, and didn't actually manage anyone who reported to him to success. His priorities were unclear, and he avoided one-on-one meetings with me. I presumed he didn't like me, and I didn't like him. Because I knew I needed to, I grudgingly worked hard at this relationship. Having been with the organization for a long time, I had had many excellent relationships with those I reported to. I had developed skills to work through issues in different cultures and became close with many of my bosses.

I always had a good understanding of what my bosses needed, and I spent time in local cultures trying to understand how people ticked so that I could both do my job better and build better relationships. I thought I was doing a pretty good job of managing up.

But I hit the wall. I thought I'd worked hard to do the right thing and build this relationship, but my wall, my personal wall, became insurmountable. I felt disrespected, and I could not stomach working with this guy. I could not fathom the actuality that—in the same company I had worked in for many years—I had to suffer under someone who didn't care about his subordinates, the work, or the work environment.

I ended up leaving the company. Although I wouldn't change anything in my career, after having spent a long time with that organization and having had so many great colleagues and clients, I still question whether I should have left because I ran into the brick wall of one bad boss. In hindsight, I know I could have done more. I could have spoken more to mentors in the organization. I should have sought coaching on how to deal with the situation.

Enough said. Don't make the same mistake.

Though I have spent time discussing both the upsides and the downsides of how you can be perceived and how you can deal with those perceptions, managing up and presenting yourself as unthreatening holds great beauty. You will build relationships with people that will last a lifetime. Everyone wants to work with and cherish those they know they can trust and count on. When trust is developed and performance is delivered, no stronger bond can form between people.

Having great relationships with people can lead to heartwarming opportunities to find true friendship and sincerity. Relationships can be built that will last a lifetime. The more deeply you work with someone, building trust together, the bigger the chance that great things will happen. And when great things happen, everyone benefits.

QUICK COACHING SESSION:

1. Do you currently consciously manage up?

2. What steps could you start taking to develop a better relationship with those who could enhance your future and become your advocates?

3. If you look realistically at your relationship with your boss, is it healthy? What can you do to make it better?

PART FIVE

SERVE OTHERS

Character is what you do when no one is watching.
—NICK SABAN

When you are alone with your thoughts and choices, you have a great opportunity to build yourself, create structure in your life, be grateful for what you have, and contemplate how to help others succeed.

Equally important, or maybe even more so, is the awareness that what you do while others are watching is paramount. Remember as you succeed and perform at high levels, people will be watching you. Many will watch you because they admire you. Many will watch you because they want to emulate you. Still others will be watching because they want to hire or promote you.

And yes, unfortunately, there will be others who will be watching you to see if you fail.

So, practice what you preach. Be a good leader. Be the kind of person people want to emulate and follow. Be the kind of person who creates opportunities for everyone you touch. Be the kind of person who cares for those around you. Balance your life between family, friends, personal time, and work.

Don't make the mistake of being one-dimensional and completely focused on work success. This does not pay. No one wants to be around at the end of their life and only be able to say, "I was really good at business."

Life has so much more to offer, and you owe it to yourself to create that so you can experience it and others can come along for the ride. Remember to be a good friend, father, mother, colleague, companion, spouse, helper, lover, mentor, and coach.

Always ask yourself and be sure of the answer to this question: Who do I serve? Dig deep and understand those constituencies and what they need to be successful. With a nuanced grasp of this answer, and those who will benefit from it, you will know what to focus on, where to put your time, and where you need to grow to become better so that you can deliver. This is a key part of leading yourself.

Early in my career, I had the H. J. Heinz Company as my client. Fresh out of business school—a confident, self-assured MBA—I had just started my first job. I could not have been more excited to learn the business and to do everything I could to help in the marketing and sale of Heinz products, namely their iconic ketchup.

As part of orientation, I went on my first business flight to Pittsburgh for introductory meetings and a plant tour. I recall being giddy on the flight from Chicago, seeing the Allegheny and Monongahela rivers for the first time, and experiencing the mountains around the city. We took a cab from the airport, and I remember anxiously arriving at the Heinz corporate offices. I'm not sure what I expected, given the history and importance of Heinz, but the humble nature of the surroundings surprised me. It looked more like a high school than corporate headquarters.

Following meetings for introductions and learning about the business, I went on a tour of the plant. My guide, a well-dressed, well-spoken older gentleman, pulled up in a sparkling clean golf cart to take me on the tour. I felt privileged to be spending time with him as he gave me his history as a lifelong Heinz employee. As a fount of knowledge about the products and how the plant worked, his impressive mastery of the company had me marveling. We visited the ketchup plant as well as other parts of the production processes in manufacturing several Heinz brands.

He introduced me to folks on the plant floor—people who were obviously his friends. They professionally explained to me the duties they performed and made a point to express their pride in working for a company that upheld such high standards of quality for their products.

Having worked summers in the steel mills in Gary, Indiana, I understood and connected with their work and their pride. I felt the same sense of pride through my colleagues there. Having the opportunity to tour the plant, learn more about Heinz, and meet the employees really capped off a great day.

When the tour finished, we needed to head back to the office and get to the airport for the return trip to Chicago.

We left in the golf cart, but the guide didn't seem to be heading back.

Instead, we took a meandering route through a neighborhood near the plant. I noticed a nice, clean piece of Americana. Children were playing, folks hung laundry in their backyards, church bells rang, and kids walked home from school.

I looked at the guide—wondering what his plans were. He stated somewhat wryly, "I bet you are wondering what we are doing in this neighborhood."

I smiled and confirmed that notion.

"This is a neighborhood where many of the Heinz employees live. These are their families—wives, husbands, children, and friends. Their wellbeing is in your hands. Your advertising sells our products. It's very important that it works."

He wanted me to know, regardless of this being my first job, regardless of my low-level tenure at the advertising agency, that the work that I did made a difference for Heinz. And maybe even more importantly, it made a difference to those folks in that neighborhood. My work would build the brand and, in the same way, create livelihoods for those who I had spoken to in the plants today.

I almost cried. It humbled and surprised me that he held my role in such high esteem. When I took the job in advertising, I thought working with well-known brands and creating business-building advertising that would be seen across the country would be an exciting ride in an exciting business. I guess I hadn't realized the real purpose lay in serving those at Heinz who worked so hard to create the products that made others' lives better.

That aha moment, brought to me by my affable Heinz tour guide, revealed my first understanding of what it means to serve others.

His polite nature and respect for me made me feel like I should move heaven and earth to serve him and the folks in that neighborhood. The power of service struck me in a profound way.

The simple power of service becomes very clear when you think beyond the job, or the product, or the role, or the company, or the money, and you start thinking about employees, customers, their lives, and what your work means to them.

It pays the mortgage. It puts kids through school. It helps people take care of elderly parents. It helps those who provide care for others. You are performing a community service in the grandest sense.

Do not allow the power of service to be lost on you.

CHAPTER 23

Inspiring Others

Life's most persistent and urgent question is, "What are you doing for others?"

—MARTIN LUTHER KING JR.

Have you ever thought about what it takes to inspire others so they follow you?

This necessitates an interesting mix of skills, emotions, and confidence. It also demands a deep understanding of what is good for others. What drives them?

When they think, "What about me?" it behooves you to know those answers.

What is in their best interest, and what can foster their development and their growth? Also, what gets them fired up about the future? If you can begin to answer some of these questions, you are well on your way to being an inspirational force.

I really had to tackle this in a challenging way in one of my companies. We were starting from scratch with our growth plan to acquire advertising agencies.

Acquisitions are difficult in the best of times. And if you read any of the literature on the success of acquisitions, you will find that most of them fail. Oftentimes they fail for different reasons, but the bottom line is that cultures clash, integration is difficult, and the employees—those being acquired as well as those in the mother company—really don't see what's in it for them. They view it as either a money play or a "get big" play or an opportunity to grow the business into different areas that don't concern or benefit them.

Those at the top in acquisition-driven businesses seldom ask the question, "What's in it for my employees?"

Given this situation and the difficulty around it, I spent a lot of time building our model, making sure the best employees in our organization as well as in the acquired organization would see value in what we were doing. I prepared my message carefully the first time I stood in front of an agency we were acquiring. I cared deeply about the principles and the employees, and I knew deep down that what we were doing created a big opportunity for them. But would they see it that way?

As I stepped in front of the group and looked into their eyes, I saw a mixture of fear, uncertainty, anxious energy, and opportunity.

Their faces were hopeful but questioning, "Who is this guy? Can I believe him?"

So, I just dug in and started speaking from my heart. I truly believed that combining our organizations would offer a big opportunity to each one of them. They would work on bigger and more sophisticated clients, and acquire new skill sets to service those larger clients. They would grow. The organization would be larger, so compensation upside and bonus opportunities would increase.

It didn't stop there. A larger company is a less risky venture, so their jobs were much more secure—and clients feel the same way. Clients always risk more by working with a smaller company, even though they oftentimes get great service and great thinking. A larger organization also produces more opportunity to meet hardworking, engaged new colleagues who would broaden their network and working relationships. They would be able to exercise creativity in a much grander way.

Working on larger clients with larger budgets would offer them the potential of engaging in more media, provide more opportunities for creativity, and grant the opportunity to move the needle for clients in a much more satisfying and interesting way on a bigger, broader stage.

We also supplied simple, practical opportunities. We could offer them better healthcare and insurance programs than the smaller company could. With a more sophisticated HR model, we were forward-thinking in terms of unlimited vacation and the opportunity to take days off for childcare and maternity leave.

In my mind, I fervently believed we were creating a brighter future for everyone.

Although I felt this built something great, I naively thought it would work for 100 percent of people. The high performers and highly engaged employees loved the opportunity. Several other folks were willing to go along with it because it sounded reasonable—although they were very worried about how everything would work.

Another group of people just didn't believe it, weren't interested, or thought a larger company would be a bureaucratic mess. Some had lived through mergers or acquisitions before. Although one could argue this is a somewhat negative approach, it contains elements of truth. Bringing two organizations together is never easy. It involves many moving parts and sometimes does not go smoothly. It takes inspiration, grit, communication, and belief.

You can't keep everyone happy. Recognizing you're never going to be 100 percent right is important. But do your research, talk to people, and find out what your team needs so you can create an authentic opportunity that will motivate everyone. Deeply understand what they want and what will inspire them.

One thing is guaranteed: It is not about you. Whether you are standing in front of your team or a larger group in your company, or having a one-on-one meeting with a key employee, remember it is only about them. The leader must figure out what's right for the organization, and what's right for the organization needs to be supported by what's right for the employees. That's the leader's job.

Remember your people are worried about job security, opportunities for them to advance, challenges, how what you say affects them, what their families will think, whether their work hours will change, how they feel about the organization, whether they believe they are being treated fairly, whether you take important diversity issues seriously, and if they believe in your vision for the future of the company.

Because that is the future of their job.

QUICK COACHING SESSION:

1. Knowing what motivates your team so you can inspire them is important. Do you understand that motivation?

   _____
   _____
   _____
   _____
   _____
   _____

2. Can you authentically stand in front of your team and speak from the heart?

   _____
   _____
   _____
   _____
   _____
   _____

3. How can you combine your vision for your team with their needs for growth, promotion, and happiness in their job?

   _____
   _____
   _____
   _____
   _____
   _____

CHAPTER 24

Remember You Are Human

No one is perfect. That's why pencils have erasers.
—WOLFGANG RIEBE

Everybody falls and must get up. How they get up when they fall is what really matters. And then they fall again. And then they get up again, and they keep trying, and they modify, and they keep trying. I'm not perfect. I couldn't write this book if I had no falls, failures, or losses. I would not have fostered any learning had I not spent time in a dark room contemplating how to be a better person—or trying to figure out a life lesson amid a painful experience.

When you go through trials and tribulations and you suffer, everyone suffers. Your family suffers, your ego suffers, your confidence suffers, and you have to figure out where your blind spots are. Spending time thinking and hashing through this to get to the other side is important. To learn from it you can't just push it away or turn a blind eye or turn your back on it. You really must go through it, entertain it, and swim through the muck.

> "When you are going through hell, keep going."
> —UNKNOWN

This is one of the truest quotes I have ever heard. When you are in the middle of something lousy, you just can't stop and forget about it. You need to keep going, get through it, learn from it, and establish the next step that takes that learning and applies it to something positive.

Being human and sharing humanity is how you show you're authentic and vulnerable. It shows how you get through the tough times and get to the other side to become the person you are destined to be.

Your organization should benefit from that authenticity. Showing weakness is important. You must be able to share the difficulties you've faced as well as those the organization is facing. The idea here is not to create worry in the minds of your people. It's to let them know you are human, and though you have the confidence to move forward, you recognize issues and are willing to have tough conversations to keep them in the loop. Through this, you will become more powerful to yourself and to others.

Being human is both wonderful and challenging. Early in my career we made five house moves in eight years. We considered ourselves very lucky to have such a wonderful and wondrous experience with our family—but boy did it take a lot of endurance, perseverance, and guts.

Making major moves for a family is one of the most stressful activities ever. Beyond the simple move, which is tough, you are experiencing an entirely new country where you need to work hard to learn the language, fit in with colleagues, learn new faces and new clients, and figure out what to shop for to prepare dinner! You also need to build friendships so that you integrate into the community at home. Your family has a life while you are at work.

I am the luckiest guy on the planet because Sue's problem-solving ability always created magical outcomes in difficult situations. Whether we were in different hospitals having our children or slogging through the momentous act of moving house, she did it with ease—all with a baby on each hip. Importantly, she built friendships and helped me build friendships in each country and neighborhood. She created our social life for me outside of the office.

When you go through things like this, humanity, gratefulness, appreciation, and love are right on the tip of your tongue. Your team will see that.

But sometimes it's not just difficult; it's downright hard. After our fifteen years in Canada, we moved back to the US. Our two youngest daughters were born in Canada to total six awesome children—and they were all growing up. We had one in college, three in high school, one in middle school, and one in elementary school.

Moving is rough on everyone, particularly on kids, regardless of their age. When we moved back to the US, one of my daughters suffered greatly. I recall ending a meeting one day and hearing my phone ring. I would usually get a call from her around lunchtime. We hadn't been living there for long, and she didn't have any friends. Being the new kid in middle school is a very tough existence. She used to go into the girls' bathroom to eat her lunch and cry. She would call and talk to me about how she felt. I cried too. Nothing produces a worse feeling than hearing my daughter suffer. I felt it viscerally.

And I know I caused it.

Although our family found getting back to the US exciting, having been born and grown up all over the world, they had never lived there and didn't really know what to expect. Well, it sucks when it culminates in a lunchtime call from the girl's bathroom where your daughter is hiding, suffering by herself so no one can see her cry.

All the kids suffered after our move from Canada to the US. They were growing up. They were teenagers trying to figure out how a different culture works. But after working their way through all this difficulty and pain, a silver lining emerged: they became immensely adaptable. They understood how to make friends, were quick to do so, and were able to quickly integrate into new schools and new neighborhoods. Though not without tears and difficulty, I believe our life path built strong kids and played a distinct role in building our strong family bond. That said, the deep humanity, the great challenges, and the emotional anxiety were sometimes overwhelming.

Now comes the business part.

Have you ever been fired? Have you ever run a business that imploded, lost clients, or borrowed too much money and couldn't repay it? Have you ever been sent in to fix something that's not fixable?

I have encountered and tried to slay all these dragons. They all came with their trials and tribulations and were big learning opportunities. They all created difficulty for me professionally and often pushed my personal life to the brink. I have always valued my family above all, but make no bones about it, I have also had to push them to the limit for my work, my career, and my drive to succeed.

As I look back over it now, I can only be grateful for the deep learning and the simple fact that I (and my marriage) survived.

I'm writing this book to walk you through the perils that I experienced, so I can help you avoid them. Over the course of the last forty years, I developed survival skills. I learned how to move money around and live on less after I got caught in a corporate political battle and got fired. I learned deep patience and belief that a window would open when the door closed. I learned to trust myself and to lean on others when the tasks were great. I really understood what building a first-class team meant, and I learned how to support them. I recognized that survival depends on a continuous learning curve and personal growth. I learned which skills were the most important ones and how to leverage them.

I also learned, mostly when the going got tough, the importance of networking and how it can really help.

When you go through these kinds of experiences, your family learns along with you. Although it isn't easy day to day, the life skills you learn through dealing with adversity are substantial.

I would really be remiss if I didn't stress how important your health is. I know we spoke about it early in the book in terms of your morning routine and making a daily workout a part of your physical and mental health. But to get through difficulties that you will without a doubt experience in your professional life, you must have a physical outlet. Whether that's yoga, riding a bike, daily workouts, lifting weights in your basement, or jogging—you simply must have it. It is nonnegotiable.

Oftentimes when you are caught in the thick of it and you are at your desk, in your car, or somewhere else where anxiety gets to you, having some tricks in your back pocket is important. I have found that breathing and meditation are great tools. You will get through it. You absolutely will. Breathing techniques and meditation can help you do so, and they will also help you reflect and learn a ton.

All this trouble is designed just for you. It's designed to make you better. It's designed to help you achieve more the next time.

It's also designed for you specifically to challenge you in this moment, with all your current strengths to make things better.

It's designed to help you see what you are missing, help you understand blind spots, and help you improve.

These so-called big problems happen *for* you, not *to* you.

So stay humble. Be human. Don't be afraid to show it. Recognize the humanity in your family and team members. Celebrate it. Others want to trust you, and they will want to be led. Your family needs to know you appreciate their sacrifice. Be capable and responsible in this way.

Acknowledge difficulty. Acknowledge opportunity. Acknowledge potential. Acknowledge tears because you will shed a whole bunch of them yourself. Inspiring others is a calling, a necessity, and an act of human kindness.

Engage someone else's mind in pursuit of a greater good.

QUICK COACHING SESSION:

1. When did you last share a difficult story that you encountered personally with a colleague?

2. Think about the last time you experienced adversity. Did you unpack it? Did you work your way through it? Have you tried to forget about it, or have you deconstructed it and tried to learn from it?

3. How did you use that adversity to inspire others?

CHAPTER 25

Be Ready to Lead

"The greatest leader is not necessarily the one who does the greatest things. He is the one that gets the people to do the greatest things."
—RONALD REAGAN

As the captain, you are the one everyone looks to for a win.

You can't do it alone; you need the team. Plus, finding ways to lead the team and inspire them to victory is a precious opportunity to help someone. In the purest sense, it's a calling.

To get there, avoid getting hung up on things that some people in charge use as badges. You are not a know-it-all. You are not someone who talks over people. You are not a throne-sitter. All these are proven ways to lose in the game of leadership.

Here are some short leadership tenets I learned in the school of hard knocks that will help you lead when the going gets tough and will be your day-to-day guide to effective leadership. You may recognize some of these from prior chapters—I want to hammer them home for you.

1. GET RID OF YOUR EGO.
The best illustration of this is an old Cherokee Nation story. A Cherokee chief told a story to his grandson about life.

"A fight is going on inside me," he said to the boy. "It is a terrible fight, and it is between two wolves. One is evil; he is anger, envy, sorrow, regret, greed, arrogance, self-pity, guilt, resentment, inferiority, lies, false pride, superiority, self-doubt, and ego.

"The other is good; he is joy, peace, love, hope, serenity, humility, kindness, benevolence, empathy, generosity, truth, compassion, and faith.

"The same fight is going on inside you and inside every other person too."

Somewhat bewildered, the grandson then asked his grandfather, "Which wolf will win?"

The old Cherokee chief simply replied, "The one you feed."

A healthy ego lives inside every leader. An ego provides personal power to get through difficult situations and daily troubles. It's an inner strength. But it must be harnessed. It must be recognized and used in the service of good. An out-of-check ego can take you down the wrong path and have you believing it's all about you.

Spend time recognizing when your ego takes over. Are you spending too much time thinking about what you want?

Conversely, consider these questions:

What's the right thing for your people?
What does your family need from you right now?
Is the next promotion or the next career move really what you want?
Is your ego driving you to more?
If you take a certain action, how will others react?

Thinking through the answer to some of these questions will help you better understand and recognize if your ego is taking over or if you've lost sight of your fundamental drive in the service of others.

2. LISTEN.

In one study, several psychotherapists were analyzed in terms of their therapeutic methodologies. The researchers found that if a person in therapy spoke about all their problems and the therapist simply exhibited warmth and repeated back what their problems were, the person in therapy believed the therapist had figured out the real issue (Moors 2017).

Believing that simply listening and understanding another person matters so greatly really is amazing. It offers the exhilarating feeling of being understood to the sufferer.

This is why listening is so powerful for a leader. Unfortunately, many leaders don't understand this. They feel like they need to have all the answers. They feel like they need to have access to all the information and share very little of it. They tend not to ask questions and, thus, listen little.

Remember, you aren't the smartest person in the room, and you don't have to be. Share and be democratic. Understand that information and data can help everyone learn and do their jobs better. Remember that one of the most powerful things you can do as a leader is to ask questions. Encourage learning within your organization. Give people credit when they take the initiative, and help others learn and build confidence.

Your style as a leader will probably change and evolve based on different situations over your career. Develop your style with support and questions and a complete dedication to listening. Repeating back what you heard is an excellent technique to use when listening. Feeling heard is often difficult, especially if there's no feedback. Enhance the person's sense that you truly heard what they said.

Few leaders listen to this extent because they think they already know the answer. In these situations, they miss the chance to both learn the small things from their team along the way and get members of their group to buy-in to opportunities. These leaders unconsciously pass on inspiring others to get on board. Most importantly, they miss the opportunity for a personal connection that shows belief in those who follow them.

People will listen to you, follow you, learn from you, appreciate you, and buy into your vision when they feel understood—not just when they understand you. If you talk at them and don't listen, you think what you're saying may be very "understandable," but you are simply not taking the time to understand them. The power comes in understanding their hopes, dreams, needs, and position—and how you can build on that to achieve your goals as a leader while helping them achieve their goals too (Katz and McNulty 1994).

Listening is the most powerful communication skill of all.

3. NEVER GIVE UP.

The character of a leader is a crucial ingredient in creating greatness within the team.

This might seem obvious. We've all seen people who are extremely focused on competition. They're totally in the game, and they never give up. They are always sweating more than everyone else. That is the crucial, never-give-up doggedness of a leader. It's who they are. It's their character driving them. These behavioral hallmarks are especially evident, whether the chips are down or they are simply getting a very difficult job done.

The greatest compliment a coach can pay an athlete is to describe them as relentless, to say they "just keep coming." This also applies in any walk of life—whether in trying to achieve your goals, in helping your family to succeed and leave a legacy, or in leading your team in sports, at church, at work, or at play. Not every team player has this quality. Some may tend to take time off or can't necessarily be counted on to be consistent. Still, others may shrink in critical situations. But this relentlessness is always evident in the leader (Walker 2017).

Leadership gets the tough jobs done. You may have seen a sporting event where a team is completely beaten. A few minutes are left in the game, and they have no way to come back and win. Some of the people on the team may have given up or are simply going through the motions to finish things off while the clock runs out.

But one player does the exact opposite. They are still pushing for speed. They are hustling like no one else on the field or court or ice. They are giving their all regardless of time left, score, or situation.

That is character. That is leadership. That says "come with me regardless of the situation because this is simply what we do and how we engage."

4. BE BOLD AND MAKE A POINT.

I have seen major corporations act boldly. Howard Schultz, CEO of Starbucks, has acted this way several times. How? He broke the cardinal rule of retailing—he shut down his stores. In 2008 Schultz deemed the product coming out of Starbucks stores no longer up to snuff. Starbucks locations were not using their proven successful methodologies uniformly, service levels were inadequate, stores weren't clean, and there was a lack of the passion needed for serving great coffee in a friendly neighborhood environment.

On February 26, he consciously shut down over 7,000 Starbucks locations to retrain the entire workforce up to the high standards of the organization, so the product would be at an exemplary level. This shocked the system and demanded excellence. This highly successful, bold step helped to kick-start and refocus the company back on the basics of its retailing vision and ultimately returned it to profitability and brand success (Schultz and Gordon 2012).

In my own little way, I did the same thing while running a small, struggling advertising agency in Europe. I took over the position of managing director to turn the organization around (turnaround number two!). Client service had struggled, and the strategic advice to clients was deteriorating. We had lost the passion for our clients' businesses and weren't focused on doing the work necessary to deliver superior marketing, thinking, and communication.

One of the most important challenges in turnaround tasks is to try to keep a major client from firing you. This new role—a twenty-four-hour-a-day job for about six months—took a toll on me and my team. We rallied often and fought a very good fight, but unfortunately, we didn't accomplish the goal. The agency lost the client—a big account.

Scorned, upset, and depleted, I sat in my office wondering what the next step could be. I thought, *Do I go out and cheerlead and say they were wrong to fire us? Or would that simply cloud the fact that we made many mistakes?* I wanted the organization, and myself, to be able to understand and learn from the mistakes that we'd made—or they would happen again.

Upon reflection, we could see we had gotten to the point where any difficulty related to serving this client became the client's fault.

They were harsh in meetings.

They didn't listen to us.

We did great work, but they couldn't see it or value it.

The client's people were subpar.

They were unable to understand our sophisticated methods and creativity.

We had gone deep down the slippery slope of believing we were right all the time. Once you start sliding, you can't get back up. Having worked long and hard at trying to reverse that slippery slope, I believed it to be our single biggest problem—and it turned out to be the nail in the coffin leading to the client loss.

So, in my own way of being bold, I shut down the company the next day (I took this action long before Howard Schultz did—just for context).

My senior team came to me, very upset with my decision, and spoke in dire terms of this mistake in judgment.

What does it say to our other clients? Don't they matter?

What if our other clients need us, and we aren't available because we are crying over spilled milk? This doesn't show resilience.

Doesn't this make a big deal of something that we don't want to publicize anyway?

These were all very good questions—ones I had spent only a minimal amount of time thinking through.

Don't miss this opportunity to understand the necessity of sitting together and analyzing what went wrong. The conclusions that we would draw from that analysis, discussion, debate, and subsequent understanding would help us better serve every other client. Each client on our roster would know we had just lost a big one. Would that make them quake in their boots? You bet it would. But I wanted our current clients to know we were committed to getting better and learning from our mistakes, to their benefit.

All our collective learning formed several conclusions about why we lost the account. Interestingly, those conclusions helped us to reestablish our proper levels of service, squarely in line with those set forth by the company's founder seventy years prior. We had simply forgotten the importance and focus of those simple ways of doing business.

So, shutting down the company and taking some time to reflect created a script to talk with those clients about how our dedication levels would be heightened in servicing them. Each one of them appreciated it. They noted feeling a bit nervous that we had lost a major account but felt confident in the future because of how we handled it.

It may not be easy, and you may be ridiculed, but moving forward with bold purpose helps you make a big impact with everyone who matters.

5. HELP OTHERS WEATHER STORMS.
When all eyes are on you, how you weather a storm is important. People are looking for signals. They derive their confidence, belief, and passionate connectivity to the company via the sense of power and strength from their leader. You will experience difficult times when you or your organization are belittled, suffer losses, or fail in the marketplace. When this happens, all eyes are on you.

In sporting terms, you need to be like Tom Brady in the final two minutes of the Super Bowl when he's ten points down: no emotion, complete focus, and complete support of the team.

You are no doubt bursting at the seams with anger, fear, emotion, or anxiety. But you can't show it.

Don't get me wrong; being an authentic leader is important. But you must be even-keeled, available, and ready for any situation—capable of creatively thinking on your feet. You can't let emotion get in your way and slow you down from the moments in which your leadership and creativity are most in demand.

How does one deal with this? Breathe deeply, go and scream or vent in the bathroom where no one can hear you, and find some place to meditate and focus. Training yourself to be nonreactive is important. Those who follow you need to have confidence in your leadership. If you are falling apart when the going gets tough, everyone and everything else will fall apart too.

If you accomplish all this, you will be a unicorn. You will be one of the select few who dedicate themselves to serving others and not allowing the moment to overtake them. Most people react to difficulty immediately and emotionally, which can create a negative chain reaction with colleagues.

Emotional control isn't easy. This muscle needs to be trained. Start by using simple meditation stress relief to help you train the muscle and understand the situation. Ideally, have a coach who you can call on to walk through issues, obstacles, and opportunities to plan action. You sometimes need a third party to keep things straight and have someone to vent to. This is for your benefit but, most importantly, is also for the benefit of others on your team—to support, serve, and help them weather storms.

Keep your ears open during a storm. You likely have very few answers, and listening to and understanding where your team is coming from will help everyone work together to come up with solutions. Remember that this situation is very difficult for them. They are thinking about themselves and are always wondering: Is the company okay? How is our leader reacting? Will I lose my job? What will that mean for my family?

Understanding where they're coming from and showing confidence in the future comes through the process of listening, encouraging, and having strong emotional control while thinking through how to create opportunity in a lousy situation.

6. BRING THE DONUTS AND CLEAN THE CONFERENCE ROOM.

Something about being willing to bring the donuts rallies everyone in your charge. It says you are willing to take on any task. It says you care. It says you can create a bit of fun and engage socially. That box of a dozen donuts says a lot about you.

You could also clean the conference room, and you could make sure the area where the team is working is loaded with the best tools to get the job done. Simply put, you are playing a supporting role to them.

Remember when I wrote about being egoless? This is where it really comes home to roost. The leader must be willing to do absolutely anything to support the team. This kind of support shows your humble nature and how appreciative you are of their efforts.

Nothing should be below you. This will garner respect and support and belief in you as a colleague. Clear their path of obstacles. The idea here is not for you to be front and center. The idea here is to let others work, let others lead, and you lead from the back. Do the work in the shadows. Meet and inspire behind the scenes. Clap people on the back. Give them support and a compliment. Recognize when someone is going through difficulty. Listen to them and help them through it. Go to lunch with them, or get a coffee. Guide them, mentor them, coach them, and support them.

This is the egoless heavy lifting that puts others first and garners untold respect for the leader.

7. BE AGGRESSIVE.

Lest you think that because I preach cleaning conference rooms and bringing donuts might mean that I don't want you to be aggressive, you are sorely mistaken. Leadership takes effort in many directions, and you need to practice them all. In an organization you solve problems, and you create opportunities by being aggressive. Move forward always.

Learn fast, reflect, get feedback, and go. Set aggressive goals and targets. Support, support, support your people, and push them to new heights. Everyone wants to achieve and is looking to you to set the path. Great achievement is never easy and certainly doesn't come by average effort. Aggressive effort with aggressive goals will always get you further.

Your people will view your aggressive nature in different ways. Bring them along, train them, support them, and give them rope, when necessary, but demand performance. Be human in tough situations and help them recognize where you are going and why you are going there. Not everyone will make it, and that's okay. But you do need to bring people along in your service as a leader to help them learn, get ahead, and reach their own goals. Even if you must let someone go who can't keep up, you can do it and still leave them with their dignity intact.

Everyone on your team will achieve if you push the rules and look for opportunities to create something new and better for your organization. I highly recommend Grant Cardone's book, *The 10X Rule*, when contemplating goal setting and managing success aggressively.

8. HAVE COURAGE.

Business isn't a spectator sport. To lead yourself and your team to success you need the courage and the confidence to take chances, to challenge conventional thinking, look around corners, make unpopular decisions, and weather difficult business conditions. The magic of having success through all this difficulty is to inspire your team to survive and thrive while doing it.

Here are a couple of simple dos and don'ts to pave the way:

Don't give up. Do get smart.

Don't blame others. Do own the problem and find solutions yourself.

Don't expect things to get better. Do engineer success.

Don't freeze from inaction. Do act, which will free up new potential. Become an action machine and you will shake loose opportunity.

Don't let issues and problems fester. Do attack problems like you attacked opportunities. The longer you let problems sit, the bigger they become. Get ahead of them while they are still small.

As Kansas City football coach Andy Reid said, *"When times are grim, be the Grim Reaper."*

When Sue and I were headed to Germany for my first overseas assignment, we really didn't know what it would be like to live a normal life there and work in that environment. We were newly married and excited to be living abroad.

After having spent eight weeks in a hotel, we finally moved into a little rental house (which, by the way, had no kitchen; the prior renter had moved out and took their kitchen, and we discovered a simple pipe coming out of the wall). We began building a new life together. Sue found work as a special education teacher at the US Army base and taught English at the Berlitz Language School. I flourished in my role, and we made lots of new friends both personally and professionally. We began to build our family.

Our eldest three children—Jack, Annika, and Tom—were born in Germany. Our full lives meant a busy and amazing time for us. We had developed our support system and found friends, and we really had our lives figured out in our new home.

But as life goes, new opportunities bubble up. Soon after we had really begun to feel at home there, a new role emerged, and the company asked me to move to Copenhagen to run the offices in Denmark and Sweden. It seemed my family and I were adventure hounds, so of course we said yes. Saying yes again brought great opportunities, great challenges, new languages, new colleagues, new clients, and new fortune to seek.

Our fourth child, Christian, came joyfully into the world in Denmark, and with him came all the love and challenge of a growing family in a new location. We loved living in Copenhagen, and I enjoyed the challenging work of turning the agency around and finding a successor. Guess what happened next?

After three years in Scandinavia, I got another phone call.

"How would you like to move to Canada and run the largest account in our Canadian company?" asked our European CEO.

Yes! Saying yes again brought wonder and challenge. Sue, eight months pregnant with our fifth child, our beautiful Sanne, again managed a cross-Atlantic move to Toronto. Upon arrival, we searched for an obstetrician in the area but had no luck. No one would accept Sue given her advanced pregnancy. After a lot of networking, phone calls, and help from the company, the nerve-wracking search ended when we were able to convince a local doctor that Sue's delivery would be easy. With our fifth, we knew the drill. The doctor begrudgingly accepted this and took Sue on as a patient.

Again, we faced a tribe of new people and a new place to live where we knew no one. Having courage is so important. Being anxious is natural, but you must deal with all this change with a smile on your face—personally and professionally. You need to take care of your family, make sure everyone's happy, and perform and face all the challenges in your job. The same challenge exists for your spouse or partner and your kids. It's not easy for anybody.

When you tackle all this and wrestle it to the ground, you can recognize the degree of grit, courage, and humility in it all. All our moving enhanced my career, and Sue and I clearly didn't lack courage—but all this pushing forward made me wonder if I had put undue strain on my family. It really worried me. Sue and I had many discussions, and we shed many tears about the difficulties associated with trying to tackle all of this.

I look back now and see how much stronger it made us both. In the moment, it seemed like we faced mountains of challenges. During our fifteen years in Canada, we proudly took Canadian citizenship. We had another daughter there, our beautiful Nicholette, bringing the total to six, our own hockey team!

Then came the call again with a different company to move back to the US. We said, "Yes!" Don't get me wrong. Each time we said yes, we had hours of conversations about the travails of the decision. We spoke to our kids, friends, and others who knew us well. We wanted to do the right thing for our family as much as for my career. This move back to the Chicago area had its own set of difficulties, even though we were moving "home," and the ones ingrained in this move were exponentially tougher. We weren't moving little kids across the world. Our kids grew up in Canada and had minds of their own. Two were in college, two were in high school, one in middle school, and one in grade school.

This new job as the global president of a different company involved a lot of travel. So, as we were trying to integrate into a new hometown, Sue shouldered the entire effort. Again, new schools, new friends, and new challenges with our teenagers added up to a very difficult family life.

Then, to make matters worse, six months into the new job a management change at corporate triggered a reorganization, and I got fired. We had just endured all the challenges, pain, and integration difficulty in the first six months of a move—with me not around very much—and the job didn't exist anymore. Therein came the immense anguish of being on the street with the demands of a growing family of eight.

This story does end well.

The time had come to move on—to start my own thing. I decided I had built enough business profit and wealth for others. The silver lining lay in the opportunity to become an entrepreneur, which launched me into the next successful chapter of my life.

Even though saying yes involved great difficulty, it always led to growth, opportunity, humility, and the potential for another step forward in life. It also helped Sue and I recognize what we were fostering in our children. They feel at home anywhere they are. They feel this way because they know how to make a home, and their mother is really the powerful icon in making that a reality, so they could viscerally feel at home. Wow, what an experience—just having gone through that story, I humbly feel so blessed with the great gratitude of having a family and a partner who could flourish with me by saying yes.

I am so happy I had the courage to say yes.

9. KNOW CLEARLY WHAT YOUR PRIORITIES ARE.

Ideally your plan drives your priorities, your goals drive your plan, and your vision drives your goals. Now, this is not corporate speak. This is personal speak. These are not words on a wall to pay lip service to. These are words, emotions, and messages tattooed on your brain that you live with to try to fulfill every minute of every day for your work, your personal life, and your family. If you get up every day knowing what your priorities are, you are way ahead of 95 percent of people on the planet.

But as you grow, achieve, and gain experience, you will find that no one can create your priorities like you can. When you lead, you need to funnel everything together for the benefit of your people. You need a vision. You need a plan. You need to set goals, and your priorities should flow from those goals so you don't get thrown off what's important.

I recall a conversation as we were trying to figure out plans to get the family back to the US for a vacation. Traveling with small children, visiting family, and navigating the myriad of hotels, rental cars, and car seats always made for a big production.

Slightly frustrated with the travel complexity, Sue blurted out, "How long are we going to have to figure things like this out? What are you working toward? What is the plan here, anyway?"

"Well, to get promoted," I replied lamely.

I sat there, completely clueless. I simply climbed the corporate ladder—really well. I hadn't been thinking much about a plan. I made things happen in each role they tossed me, and the successes were piling up—at least, job wise.

I had become very successful at managing difficult situations where courage, decision making, and thinking on my feet created success. But back to the original question… No, I did not have a plan.

When someone else had a plan, I easily executed it. When I woke up in the morning back then, somebody else set the priorities and told me what city to solve a problem in. I solved it. I achieved. But as my family grew and I gained stature in the organization, strategic planning of my career for the benefit of my family became more important.

In my coaching, this is the toughest thing to accomplish with my clients. They're so busy that their workday takes over. Important potential opportunities fall prey to the immediate needs, whether important or not. Do not allow this to happen. Know your priorities. Write them down and have them in front of your face before you go to bed at night and in the morning when you wake up. Don't let your well-conceived and meticulously crafted priorities fall prey to the urgent.

QUICK COACHING SESSION:

1. How good of a listener are you? Answer this truthfully and take immediate action.

2. Do you expect others to bring the donuts and clean the conference room?

3. When the going gets tough, can you stay even-keeled? The next time you and your team encounter difficulty, how could you act differently to foster more confidence and belief in your leadership?

CHAPTER 26

See the Future and Paint the Picture

A vision is not just a picture of what could be; it is an appeal to our better selves, a call to become something more.
—ROSABETH MOSS KANTER

Visionary is a loaded word. It has a lot of definitions, and many different types of people who embody them are indeed "visionary." But the fact is, in business and in life, everyone is inspired by *seeing their place* in the future. It gives them the opportunity to see opportunity. It allows them to believe that better things are coming for them. It helps them to have confidence in the future and enhances their desire to follow the type of people who can paint the picture.

Most importantly, a vision for the future helps people to understand where they will fit in. They can see where they are in the picture you are painting. They can see growth in themselves. They can ascertain how this is good for their family. And from a personal perspective, it helps them understand your mission and helps them buy-in.

When you paint the picture of the future, and it's clear, the stress of "Where are we going?" and "Why are we going there?" and "Why are we doing this anyway?" is gone. Your mind and others can be flush with the ideas and opportunities and the thinking necessary to make the future happen.

The need to survive is a basic human instinct. A vision for the future is a picture of that survival. It creates solidarity and a place where team members can come together to help create that picture. Power is in numbers. You exponentiate your vision by sharing that vision and leading others to help you create it.

Some will think differently or won't buy-in to your vision of the future. This is normal, and you should expect it. Folks come to work with their own set of beliefs, and that's okay. Your job is to get them on board. Recognize that your vision might mean substantial changes for them. That's not easy. In the end, many will buy-in; some will not.

You may have to endure some pain as that lack of support manifests itself. Recognize that is part of leadership. Respect those who can't or won't buy-in to your vision, and encourage them to find opportunity elsewhere. Everyone deserves the right to work where they believe in the outcome and can derive personal satisfaction.

As respectful as one can be of another's perspective, you might occasionally come across someone with a bad attitude.

A person in an organization with a bad attitude, who lacks belief in the vision or the company, can create chaos within it.

You may have to fight for your vision.

I took over a small Canadian agency that needed to be turned around (my third!). It suffered, financially and culturally. Folks weren't being treated with much respect, and the work environment showed it. I needed to step in and establish clear rules of engagement for what would be tolerated and what wouldn't be. I also laid out my vision for how I believed we could leverage talent within the organization to move forward and find success.

Within a short period, as I got to know my staff, one individual did not buy-in to where we were headed. She didn't believe in the vision, and she didn't like the changes I'd made. She walked around the office assembling small groups of employees, telling them she "believed the company was going to go under," adding that "John's leadership is not going to save us. It makes no sense to believe anything he says."

I had never encountered anything like this before. Sure, I had seen and experienced unhappy employees, but only in larger businesses, and even then the voices were faint. This small agency, on the verge of failing, heard every voice. Unfortunately, the unhappy senior leader had a large team. I had to get to the bottom of it.

I called her in my office to better understand the issue, in hopes that I might be able to repair things. Although she had been caustic when speaking to team members, she acted very pleasant toward me. She told me she worried about the future of the company, given its difficult past. That made sense to me. She really cared and apologized for any problems she may have caused in speaking to others.

I walked her through my plan and why I thought it would work. She seemed open-minded.

Unfortunately, that open-mindedness didn't last long. She continued her caucuses in the office.

We sat down again. This time, I delivered my respectful message in a more straightforward manner. "I'm sorry, Jennifer, but if you are going to continue bad-mouthing the company and me, while belittling others who want to make a go of this, this organization may not be a great place for you to contribute."

She responded, somewhat surprised, "Oh, I'm so sorry. My perspectives have clearly been taken out of context. Although I am worried about where the company is headed, I am fully on board."

We discussed this more, and it became obvious that she enjoyed manipulating me—big time.

Weirdly, this didn't bother me. It was her vocal disagreement with my vision for the organization that created my uneasiness. I didn't want Jennifer sowing seeds of discontent. I wanted her to believe, but that didn't seem to be in the cards.

Running a company when everything is running reasonably well is tough enough. Trying to turn things around while pushing back against folks who vocally don't believe and are trying to influence others is much more difficult—even if it's just one.

I doubled down on my communication to everyone in the company and made sure that I listened to and addressed others who had different perspectives. In doing so I learned a thing or two. I found I could mold my vision and align it with those who could engage in the process, make it better, and play a positive role going forward.

Jennifer did very good work. As an engaged leader, her team liked her. That made this struggle even more difficult. I needed to have my senior people on board, and I really needed her skill set in the company.

Unfortunately, her backstabbing continued. Late one afternoon, word got back to me that she had engaged a group of employees in an open area of the office.

I walked over to where she spoke to the assembly and asked her politely to join me in my office. As I walked past our HR leader, I asked her to join us as well. I needed to have a third-party witness this, as I didn't have any idea how she would react.

My worst fears were confirmed.

"You f*cking American!" Jennifer screamed. "If HR wasn't here, I would throw open the door of your office and scream *rape*! You can't fire me! If you do, this place will go down! I'm too important! My lawyer will bankrupt you. I am a single mother, you f*cker!"

Completely aghast, but somehow maintaining my composure, I told her that her actions had created an untenable situation. Clearly, her employment with us had no future. I let her go.

As I personally walked her back to her desk to get her things, she continued shouting obscenities and called for others to follow her out the door as she left.

No one did.

Leadership is tough. Sometimes people don't agree with you or the vision you have created. Sometimes they are vocal. Other times they self-select and quit. Occasionally, disagreement is violent, like in my personal story above. Though it's challenging, creating a vision for the future is your most powerful way to serve others. It creates a self-perpetuating livelihood for them and a future for their families. They can see that their own aspirations and growth are in the forefront of your mind. That is the greatest and most powerful part of leadership.

A particularly fun part of painting the picture and creating vision of a company is achieving it! As you climb the mountain and achieve the goals, you must consistently motivate your team with thanks and celebration of accomplishments.

The simple act of addressing this breeds gratitude every day for you and your team.

Research has proven that celebrating and enunciating gratitude brings belief, confidence, and a powerful mindset (Portocarrero 2020). Nothing beats a good celebration! Your people know you care and can see you in a different light than during your day-to-day leadership. Celebrate them. Celebrate your family for supporting you. Celebrate your colleagues who help you achieve. Send a note to someone who mentored you, and celebrate their guidance that made you a better person.

Lastly, celebrate yourself for your dedication to learning, growing, and new experiences. Celebrate mistakes, successes, stubbing your toe, or landing flat on your face. All this becomes who you are. Put in the right frame, it is a beautiful picture of gratitude, humility, service, and success.

QUICK COACHING SESSION:

1. Have you painted a picture of the future for those you lead? Have you painted that picture for yourself?

   _____
   _____
   _____
   _____
   _____
   _____

2. Are you consistently communicating your vision to your team? Are you getting buy-in?

   _____
   _____
   _____
   _____
   _____
   _____
   _____

3. Name three things you could celebrate with your family, yourself, and your team.

   _____
   _____
   _____
   _____
   _____
   _____
   _____

CHAPTER 27

The Helpless CEO

The CEO role is about serving others so they perform at the highest levels—not doing their job for them.

A leader that I've mentored had just taken his first CEO job. After a short honeymoon period in the job, I started working with him. He knew the demands were substantial, and his confidence and excitement about being in charge buoyed him.

That said, he seemed confused and slightly distraught. He felt helpless. He had progressed his way through the organization by performing at super-high levels. When he took over sales and managed the team, the organization had record results. When he took over the head of marketing role, the organization expanded its marketing breadth and built its brand substantially.

This organization created notable, highly creative marketing campaigns. When he oversaw product development, the company enjoyed great success with substantial and successful launches. They expanded their product line far beyond what had previously existed, and this loaded the organization for future growth. This individual had built on positive experiences at each step in his career.

Now, as the CEO, why did he feel helpless? He felt this way because he "wasn't doing anything." He normally spent his time creating work that moved the business forward, whether working on marketing campaigns, making sales calls to large organizations, or developing new products.

Prior to becoming CEO, he spent his time "doing." While *doing*, he felt engaged, involved, and part of the team. While *doing*, he could hold something in his hand and understand his contribution. While *doing*, he felt like he had accomplished something. Now, as a "helpless CEO," he felt lost from not doing.

This is an interesting quandary. A high performer—so good, in fact, that he had been named CEO—felt like he could not accomplish anything in his new role.

Understanding the dilemma and feeling empathy for him, I posed a couple questions.

"How do you feel about your team?"

He replied with a smile, "I'm quite excited about the quality and diversity of my direct reports. I think my group is positively positioned to grow the organization."

"Well," I said, "okay… If one of those team members came to you with a problem or a serious roadblock, what would you do?"

Confidence spread across his features. "I'll sit down with them and work through the problem. We'll brainstorm some solutions. Or I could help them with some direction, so we can work through some solutions together."

Great!

"If one of those team members came to you and asked for some time off because they had a serious family situation or a death in the family, how would you respond?"

He responded quickly and clearly, "I'll support them. I'll give them the time off and call the group together so we can fill in, so no one misses a beat." I could tell he really wanted to take care of his team.

My next question dug a little deeper. "If your head of product development came to you, struggling with a regulatory roadblock or facing difficulty getting around a particular issue in the testing phase, what would you do?"

He smiled as he started to figure out my line of questioning.

"Well, I would help him work through the issues. And if there were any roadblocks that he encountered that I could help him with, I would try to clear them for him."

Lastly, I asked, "If a part of your organization didn't make their numbers and were under performing, what would you do?"

He answered thoughtfully: "I would sit down with them. I would want to understand their struggle. I know everyone on my team operates with the best intentions, so I would try to get under the surface to discover issues that were holding them back. I would want them to make the decisions necessary to move forward, but if I could shine some light on difficult issues to help them engage, I would try to help."

Does this sound like a helpless CEO, or does it sound like an empathetic colleague who wants to drive performance, lead team members, remove roadblocks, and offer help?

His actions were right on. He acted as a leadership-oriented CEO using the skills he developed as a high performer in the organization, leading different departments, and helping others perform. He had learned to serve. And by serving others, he had served the company and himself. He now enjoyed the ultimate role of service as the head of the organization.

When you lead, you are serving others. The doing is in the serving. He made up the problem in his mind. And once we had this discussion, his mind opened to an entirely new state. He serves by *doing*.

As a leader in any organization—whether at the bottom, the middle, or the top—your role is to serve others. Sometimes that serving is related to performing a task. Other times that serving entails thoughtfully guiding people and helping them navigate a problem. Serving others is leading.

Following our session, we laughed that the notion a CEO is helpless because they are not doers, even though that's how they got the job. The power is in the mind, and in particular, powerful minds learn how to serve.

Although it might seem odd that one might view a CEO as helpless, on the surface it can look that way. They technically don't do anything. They have financial specialists to take care of the numbers, salespeople to do the selling, marketing people to do the marketing, project managers to manage projects, and software engineers to manage and execute software builds and integration.

They do, however, have the ultimate responsibility and accountability for the organization and the decisions made on its behalf. They are accountable for the company's health, in every way. Their job is to motivate, inspire, and lead team members to performance with excellence, creating prosperity and opportunity for everyone. Their job is to solve problems, remove roadblocks, and push the organization through rough patches. Their job is also to admit mistakes, change course, and plot a new direction for everyone when necessary.

That's a lot of responsibility for someone who doesn't *do anything.*

* * *

So, you want to be a CEO.

I applaud your drive, ambition, and initiative to learn what it takes to get there. The journey has ups and downs, but it's a lot of fun. Taking risks, learning, succeeding, leading, and building confidence are exciting milestones on your career path when you stretch to get to the top. Though failing and making mistakes is no fun, even the worst failures are rich in learning opportunities and can launch you into new thought patterns that will help you succeed at entirely different levels. You will be amazed at how the sky can open when you are thinking through the how and why you screwed up.

I hope I have made my version of the path to CEO clear. I have tried to be authentic and honest about my highs and lows as well as the steps I took to create my path. I also wanted to outline areas where I proved deficient or needed more learning and experience—as well as areas where my know-it-all attitude got me into trouble.

I created what I believe are the five most important areas of development in getting to CEO:

- Self-awareness
- Performance routine
- Run to the fire
- Manage up
- Serve others

I feel these are the most powerful areas of learning that are necessary to track my path as well as to imagine yourself in yours. They are chock-full of methods, stories, and opportunities for you to put yourself in my shoes and create your own plan.

I wanted you to know what worked for me and what didn't. I also want you to learn from my mistakes. Where I have read great books about how to succeed, I took note of and listed them. My sincere interest is to have you feel like you can use this as a guidebook on your leadership journey.

Lastly, I wanted to say two more words about mistakes:

Make them.

Everybody does. And every CEO made many of them on their path to the top job. You won't get fired. You will learn.

Don't be afraid to take calculated risks and learn from the inevitable twists and turns.

Making and analyzing my mistakes offered me the humblest learning of my career. Some mistakes were quite painful, others quite small and insignificant. But the learning I garnered from them created new opportunity for me. This, in turn, made me better at my job from day to day and pushed, prodded, and helped me get promoted.

My biggest errors created such profound learning experiences that they helped me see things I *never* would have otherwise seen.

And, as you read in this book, that kind of learning helped me save my marriage.

In a logical way, the more mistakes you make, the more learning you get; the faster you make them, the quicker you can achieve greatness.

Go achieve greatness.

Start Your Journey Reading List

As an aspiring CEO, you can read several books to learn how to navigate toward and keep the top job. Here are some of the must reads:

Good to Great, by Jim Collins—this book analyzes the traits that set great companies apart from good ones and teaches how to take your company from good to great.

The 7 Habits of Highly Effective People, by Stephen Covey—this book covers seven principles for success that can be applied to both personal and professional life.

The Hard Thing About Hard Things, by Ben Horowitz—this book provides insights on how to manage the tough decisions and challenges that come with being a CEO.

Leaders Eat Last, by Simon Sinek—this book explores how great leaders create a culture of trust and cooperation within their organizations.

The 21 Irrefutable Laws of Leadership, by John C. Maxwell—this book distills leadership down to a handful of principals to enhance your life.

How to Win Friends and Influence People, by Dale Carnegie—this classic book provides timeless principles for building relationships, communicating effectively, and inspiring others.

The Captain Class: A New Theory of Leadership, by Sam Walker—using deep research into the best sports teams of all time, the author uncovers the simple yet surprising leadership traits of the captains that made the teams unstoppable.

The 5AM Club: Own Your Morning. Elevate Your Life, by Robin Sharma—this book explores the life-changing advantages of a world-class morning routine and how it sets you up for success in your work and your life.

The CEO Next Door, by Elena L. Botelho and Kim R. Powell—this book outlines a research study of over 2,600 leaders to reveal their best practices.

The 10X Rule: The Only Difference Between Success and Failure, by Grant Cardone—Cardone pushes you to exceed expectations by setting goals ten times greater than you think you can achieve.

Shoe Dog, by Phil Knight—the longtime founder and CEO of Nike tells his personal struggles and the story of Nike's rise to global brand leadership.

Extreme Ownership: How U.S. Navy SEALs Lead And Win, by Jocko Willink and Leif Babin—this book emphasizes the importance of taking full responsibility for every aspect of one's life and working to achieve greater success and overcome challenges.

Acknowledgments

Beginning an undertaking like this is immediately humbling. It's one thing to start pulling the thoughts out of your head and another to put them down in words. And still another, to assure they will be of value to others.

As I recounted my learning, stories, mistakes, and triumphs, I quickly recognized that the positive attitude of my wife, Sue, and my children were the genesis of each one of these opportunities.

Sue and our children, Jack, Annika, Tom, Christian, Sanne, and Nicholette, toughed out five moves to different countries, new houses, and unfamiliar neighborhoods, all while making new friends, getting on new sports teams, and figuring out new schools—because Dad took a new job to create a better life. They suffered, they grew, and they are benefitting from that growth today. I am humbly and deeply grateful to them. I have also been made a better man by becoming "Pops." I have my lovely granddaughters, Savannah and Adeline, to thank for that.

I started this book with very little knowledge of how to do so. My long-time friend Dan Doster encouraged me often to get started. I eventually got connected to Eric Koester at Georgetown University and Manuscripts through Deborah Crowe after having connected with Deb on LinkedIn. What a small world. The Manuscripts folks are an incredible group of publishers who walk you through the process with smarts, thoughtfulness, and patience.

Thanks to my developmental editor Ty Mall, who got me off the ground with his valuable feedback. Whitney McGruder, my revisions editor, prodded me in her nice, sweet voice to systematically upgrade my writing to her high expectations. I appreciate Venus Bradley and Chanda Elaine Spurlock for their feedback on my first draft. Thanks to Gjorgji Pejkovski, Nikola Tikoski, and Simona Gjurovska, for cover design, copy editors Michelle Felich and Bill Badi, and marketing specialists Stephanie McKibben and John Chancey. Manuscripts folks behind the scenes popped up to enhance my writing process, and I am grateful to each: Sherman Morrison, Jordan Waterwash, Kristy Carter, Shawna Quigley, Kyra Ann Dawkins, Chuck Oexmann, Kayla LeFevre, Eldar Huseynov, among others, thank you.

My leadership journey got a serious upgrade when I joined the Young President's Organization (YPO). I have benefitted from the interaction with presidents in this organization for over twenty years. Each of my four YPO Forums created not only the opportunity to become a better CEO but also to form deep friendships.

I would particularly like to thank Mark Springer, Jon Evans, KC Tolliver, Kelly Coleman, Rick Ungersma, Rex Leipheimer, Joe Brandt, Blake Underriner, and Kevin Cook in Big Sky Forum 5 for continuing to push my learning envelope.

I would also like to thank past forum mates Jim Leopardo, Peter Garvy, Tom Kotel, Matt Alagna, Bill Best, Mitch Wilneff and Ed Benford, for your help and guidance.

My early days as a CEO were fortified by my Toronto forum mates Mike Meagher, Robert Hashimoto, Graeme Jewett, Mitch Massicotte, Greg McKenzie, Salim Manji, Joe Chesham, and Brian Read. Thanks also to those who valued my guidance: George Pimentel, David LeCompte, Matt McDonnell, Fred Kendall, and Vu Pham. Rick Davis and Bruce Leslie keep me on track with our weekly check-ins. Curtis Brackenbury and Scott Robinson helped me develop my signature.

My early mentors at Leo Burnett were Hank Feeley, Kerry Rubie, Jim Jenness, Bill Lynch, Achim Schulz, and Reiner Erfert. I learned a ton at The Marketing Store Worldwide from Graham Kemp and Dave Tridle. Thanks to Mark Anthony for teaming up with me on our entrepreneurial journey.

I very much appreciate the guidance and insight of my friend and leadership coach Robin Sharma.

Internet ventures were a tough ride but provided great learning with Hart Hillman. Early leadership roles were enhanced by my camaraderie with Allen Chichester, Steve Simmons,

Mark Eden, Bonnie Hillman, Klaus Hahn, Carl Unger, Frank Eigler, Stefan Jung, and Beate Jung-Meyer.

Special thanks to my brother Dan Hilbrich, an early, caring, faithful, and patient investor.

Lastly, I want to thank my mom and dad, Jack and Judie Hilbrich, who emboldened me with the confidence, support, and time to help me develop into the person I am. I care about others because they cared deeply about me. As the oldest of eight, I always had support from my seven siblings: Dan, Ruthanne, Genna, Judy, Amy, Jill, and Tom. Thank you all for your love and for being there to make me and our family strong.

Appendix

INTRODUCTION

Botelho, Elena L., Kim R. Powell, and Tahl Raz. 2018. *The CEO Next Door: The 4 Behaviors That Transform Ordinary People into World-Class Leaders*. New York, NY: Currency.

Sharma, Robin. 2018. *The 5AM Club: Change Your Morning, Change Your Life*. London: Harper Thorsons.

CHAPTER 1: GOALS

Cardone, Grant. 2011. *The Ten X Rule: The Only Difference Between Success and Failure*. Hoboken, NJ: Wiley.

Doran, George T. 1981. "There's a S.M.A.R.T. Way to Write Management's Goals and Objectives." *Management Review* 70, no. 11 (1981): pp. 35–36. https://community.mis.temple.edu/mis-0855002fall2015/files/2015/10/S.M.A.R.T-Way-Management-Review.pdf.

Sharma, Robin. 2018. *The 5AM Club: Change Your Morning, Change Your Life*. London: Harper Thorsons.

Ziglar, Zig. 2019. *Goals: How to Get the Most out of Your Life*. Shippensburg: Sound Wisdom.

CHAPTER 2: REALISTICALLY ASSESS YOUR SKILLS

Everything DiSC. "Wiley Everything Disc Solutions." John Wiley & Sons, Inc. Accessed on January 3, 2023. https://www.everythingdisc.com/.

Gallup, Inc. "Live Your Best Life Using Your Strengths." Gallup. Accessed on January 3, 2023. https://www.gallup.com/cliftonstrengths/en/home.aspx.

CHAPTER 3: WHAT IS YOUR SUPERPOWER?

Linsky, Marisa. 2019. "20 Motivational Quotes for Finals Week." *The Cabrini Blog* (blog) Cabrini University. https://www.cabrini.edu/blog/2019-20-posts/inspiring-quotes.

CHAPTER 4: WHAT DOES SUCCESS MEAN TO YOU?

Alarm, Asloob. "82 Motivational Productivity Quotes That Will Alter Your Stance." *Troop Messenger* (blog). February 16, 2023. https://www.troopmessenger.com/blogs/productivity-quotes.

CHAPTER 5: WHAT DRIVES YOUR SUCCESS?

Leadem, Rose. 2017. "10 Coco Chanel Quotes to Push You Towards Success." *Entrepreneur* (blog). May 18, 2017. https://www.entrepreneur.com/leadership/10-coco-chanel-quotes-to-push-you-towards-success/294230.

CHAPTER 6: HOW DO YOU INFLUENCE OTHERS?
BYU Speeches. "Carl W. Buehner." Brigham Young University. Accessed on February 6, 2023. https://speeches.byu.edu/speakers/carl-w-buehner/.

Dalio, Ray. 2017. *Principles*. New York, NY: Simon & Schuster.

Evans, Richard L. 1976. *Richard Evans' Quote Book*. Salt Lake City, UT: Publishers Press.

CHAPTER 8: ESTABLISH HIGH PRODUCTIVITY
Auden, W. H. 1958. *The Life of a That-There Poet*. New York, NY: New Yorker.

Canal, Emily. 2017. "3 Killer Lessons from Stephen King's Insanely Productive Writing." *Inc. Magazine* (blog). September 12, 2017. https://www.inc.com/emily-canal/stephen-king-it-movie-box-office.html.

Currey, Mason. 2013. "Benjamin Franklin." In *Daily Rituals: How Artists Work*. 385–402. New York, NY: Knopf.

Currey, Mason. 2013. "Wolfgang Amadeus Mozart." In *Daily Rituals How Artists Work*. 323–41. New York, NY: Knopf.

Fig, Joe. 2009. *Inside the Painter's Studio*. New York: Princeton Architectural Press, New York.

Sharma, Robin. 2018. *The 5AM Club: Change Your Morning, Change Your Life.* London: Harper Thorsons.

Sielski, Mike. 2022. *The Rise: Kobe Bryant and the Pursuit of Immortality.* London, UK: Macmillan.

CHAPTER 9: LEARN AND DON'T STOP LEARNING

Maxwell, John C. 2022. *The 15 Invaluable Laws of Growth: Live Them and Reach Your Potential.* New York, NY: Center Street.

Meah, Asad. 2016. "34 Motivational Andrew Carnegie Quotes." *Awaken The Greatness Within* (blog). July 8, 2016. https://www.awakenthegreatnesswithin.com/34-motivational-andrew-carnegie-quotes/.

Sharma, Robin. 2018. *The 5AM Club: Change Your Morning, Change Your Life.* London: Harper Thorsons.

CHAPTER 10: PAUSE AND REFLECT

Ohgami, Katsuki. 2019. *366 Buddhist Proverbs: A Year of Practical Buddhism for Happiness, Meditation and Enlightenment.* Self-published.

CHAPTER 11: DON'T BE THE SMARTEST PERSON IN THE ROOM

Nielsen, Dan. "Franklin D. Roosevelt Quotes." *Presidential Leadership* (blog). Accessed on January 29, 2023. https://presidentialleadershipbook.com/franklin-roosevelt/quotes/.

Smith, Don. 2022. "You Are the Average of the Five People You Spend the Most Time with – Jim Rohn." *Personal Growth Channel* (blog). September 1, 2022. https://www.personal-growthchannel.com/2018/07/you-are-average-of-five-people-you.html.

CHAPTER 12: MEASURE YOUR PERFORMANCE

Martin, Thomas-Henri. 1868. *Galilée, Les Droits De La Science Et La méthode Des Sciences Physiques, Par Th.-Henri Martin.* Paris, France: Didier.

CHAPTER 13: GETTING UNSTUCK

Disney. 2018. "5 Inspiring Walt Disney Quotes." *Disney News* (blog). October 1, 2018. https://news.disney.com/inspiring-walt-disney-quotes/.

CHAPTER 14: RUN TO THE FIRE

Sinek, Simon. 2014. "Why Good Leaders Make You Feel Safe." Filmed March 2014 in Vancouver, Canada. TED video, 11:01. https://www.ted.com/talks/simon_sinek_why_good_leaders_make_you_feel_safe/c.

CHAPTER 15: WHICH FIRES DO I RUN TO?

Churchill, Winston. 2021. "Fight on the Beaches." *International Churchill Society* (blog). September 13, 2021. https://winstonchurchill.org/resources/quotes/we-shall-fight-on-the-beaches-2/.

Coaching for Leaders Staff. "3 Steps to Sounding Like Someone Who Gets Promoted. *Coaching for Leaders* (blog). Innovate Learning, LLC. Accessed on January 29, 2023. https://coachingforleaders.com/someone-who-gets-promoted/.

JayMJ23. 2006. "Michael Jordan 'Failure' Nike Commercial." JayMJ23. August 25, 2006. 00:30. https://youtube.com/watch?v=45mMioJ5szc&feature=shares.

Rotella, Robert J. and Robert Cullen. 2004. *Golf Is Not a Game of Perfect*. London, UK: Simon & Schuster.

The Moth. "The Art and Craft of Storytelling." *The Moth*. Accessed February 11, 2023. https://themoth.org/.

CHAPTER 16: CHOOSE YOUR TEAM CAREFULLY

Collins, Jim. 2001. *Good to Great Why Some Companies Make the Leap… and Others Don't*. New York, NY: HarperCollins.

CHAPTER 17: SAY YES AND FIGURE IT OUT

Branson, Richard. 2017. *Finding My Virginity: The New Autobiography*. London, UK: Virgin Books.

CHAPTER 18: CONFRONT STUFF, LOOK AROUND CORNERS, AND BELIEVE

Hadfield, Chris. 2014. *You Are Here: Around the World in 92 Minutes*. Toronto, Ontario: Random House Canada.

McGrath, Rita Gunther. 2021. *Seeing Around Corners: How to Spot Inflection Points in Business Before They Happen.* Boston, MA: Mariner Books.

Rogers, Heather. 2007. "Current Thinking." *The New York Times.* June 3, 2007. https://www.nytimes.com/2007/06/03/magazine/03wwln-essay-t.html.

Solar House History. 2013. "Edison's Famous Quote." *Solar House History* (blog). February 28, 2013. http://solarhousehistory.com/blog/2013/2/28/edisons-famous-quote.

PART FOUR: MANAGE UP

Rousmaniere, Dana. 2015. "What Everyone Should Know about Managing Up." *Harvard Business Review* (blog). January 23, 2015. https://hbr.org/2015/01/what-everyone-should-know-about-managing-up.

CHAPTER 20: DON'T LET YOUR EGO GET THE BEST OF YOU

Smith, Thomas. 2023. "55 Ego Quotes to Stop Being Selfish or Egocentric." *Happier Human* (blog). March 2, 2023. https://www.happierhuman.com/ego-quotes/.

CHAPTER 21: KNOW YOUR NUMBERS

Platonic Realms. "Plato." *Platonic Realms* (blog). Accessed on January 30, 2023. https://platonicrealms.com/quotes/Plato.

PART FIVE: SERVE OTHERS

Saban, Nick and Brian Curtis. 2007. *How Good Do You Want to Be?: A Champion's Tips on How to Lead and Succeed at Work and in Life*. New York City: Random House Publishing Group.

CHAPTER 23: INSPIRING OTHERS

King Jr., Martin Luther. 1963. *Strength to Love by Martin Luther King Jr., Sermon: Three Dimensions of a Complete Life*. New York, NY: Harper & Row.

CHAPTER 24: REMEMBER YOU ARE HUMAN

Riebe, Wolfgang. 2011. *A Further 100 Quotes to Make You Think*. Wolfgang Riebe. Apple Books.

CHAPTER 25: BE READY TO LEAD

Cardone, Grant. 2011. *The Ten X Rule: The Only Difference Between Success and Failure*. Hoboken, NJ: Wiley.

Foote, Jordan. 2022. "Andy Reid on His Message to Patrick Mahomes: 'When It's Grim, Be the Grim Reaper.'" *FanNation* (blog). *Sports Illustrated*. January 24, 2022. https://www.si.com/nfl/chiefs/gameday/kc-chiefs-coach-andy-reid-on-his-message-to-patrick-mahomes-when-its-grim-be-the-grim-reaper.

Katz, Neil and Kevin McNulty. 1994. "Reflective Listening." Syracuse University. Accessed on February 3, 2023. https://www.maxwell.syr.edu/docs/default-source/ektron-files/reflective-listening-nk.pdf?sfvrsn=f1fa6672_5.

Moors, François and Emmanuelle Zech. 2017. "The Effects of Psychotherapist's and Clients' Interpersonal Behaviors During a First Simulated Session: A Lab Study Investigating Client Satisfaction." *Frontiers in Psychology* 8. (Oct 2017). https://doi.org/10.3389/fpsyg.2017.01868.

Reagan, Ronald. "Leadership." *The Ronald Reagan Presidential Foundation & Institute*. Accessed April 10, 2023. https://www.reaganfoundation.org/education/e-learning/leadership/.

Schultz, Howard and Joanne Gordon. 2011. *Onward: How Starbucks Fought for Its Life without Losing Its Soul*. New York, NY: Rodale.

Yeo, Alyssa. 2016. "The Story of Two Wolves." *Urban Balance* (blog). February 24, 2016. https://www.urbanbalance.com/the-story-of-two-wolves/.

Walker, Sam. 2018. *The Captain Class: A New Theory of Leadership*. New York, NY: Random House.

CHAPTER 26: SEE THE FUTURE AND PAINT THE PICTURE

Kanter, Rosabeth Moss. 2005. "Confidence: How Winning Streaks and Losing Streaks Begin and End." *International Journal of Productivity and Performance Management* 54, no. 3 (April 2005). https://doi.org/10.1108/ijppm.2005.07954cae.003.

Portocarrero, Florencio F., Katerina Gonzalez, and Michael Ekema-Agbaw. 2020. "A Meta-Analytic Review of the Relationship between Dispositional Gratitude and Well-Being." *Personality and Individual Differences* 164 (2020): 110101. https://doi.org/10.1016/j.paid.2020.110101.

Made in the USA
Monee, IL
16 June 2023

36015011R00149